First World War

and Army of Occupation

War Diary

France, Belgium and Germany

38 DIVISION
113 Infantry Brigade
Royal Welsh Fusiliers
13th Battalion
1 December 1915 - 30 April 1919

WO95/2555/1

The Naval & Military Press Ltd
www.nmarchive.com
Published in association with The National Archives

Published by

The Naval & Military Press Ltd

Unit 10 Ridgewood Industrial Park,

Uckfield, East Sussex,

TN22 5QE England

Tel: +44 (0) 1825 749494

www.naval-military-press.com

www.nmarchive.com

This diary has been reprinted in facsimile from the original. Any imperfections are inevitably reproduced and the quality may fall short of modern type and cartographic standards.

Contents

Document type	Place/Title	Date From	Date To
Heading	WO95/2555/1 13 Battalion Royal Welsh Fusiliers		
Heading	38th Division 113th Infy Bde 13th Bn Roy. Welsh Fus. Dec 1915-Apr 1919		
Heading	38th Division 113/38 13th R.W. Fus. Vol I Dec. 15		
War Diary	Winchester	01/12/1915	01/12/1915
War Diary	Havre	02/12/1915	03/12/1915
War Diary	Ecques	11/12/1915	11/12/1915
War Diary	Pont Du Hem	12/12/1915	18/12/1915
War Diary	L.E Sart	19/12/1915	31/12/1915
Heading	38th Div. 13th R.W. Fus. Vol 2 Jan 16		
War Diary	Le Sart	01/01/1916	04/01/1916
War Diary	Le Sart in Kings Road	05/01/1916	18/01/1916
War Diary	Forward Area	19/01/1916	08/02/1916
War Diary	Locon	08/02/1916	16/02/1916
War Diary	Givenchy	17/02/1916	29/02/1916
Heading	13 RW Fus Vol 4 March 1916		
War Diary	Gorre	01/03/1916	03/03/1916
War Diary	Trenches in Givenchy	04/03/1916	08/03/1916
War Diary	Les Choquans	09/03/1916	16/03/1916
War Diary		15/03/1916	15/03/1916
War Diary	Festubert	16/03/1916	20/03/1916
War Diary	Front Line Trenches Festubert	21/03/1916	24/03/1916
War Diary	Le Touret	25/03/1916	28/03/1916
War Diary	Front Line Trenches	28/03/1916	31/03/1916
War Diary	Festubert	01/04/1916	01/04/1916
War Diary	Les Choquaux	02/04/1916	07/04/1916
War Diary	Givenchy Les-la-Banes	09/04/1916	15/04/1916
War Diary	Les Choquaux	16/04/1916	16/04/1916
War Diary	Laventie	17/04/1916	20/04/1916
War Diary	Pont Du Hem	21/04/1916	24/04/1916
War Diary	Robermetz	24/04/1916	30/04/1916
War Diary	Laventie	01/05/1916	02/05/1916
War Diary	Fauquisart	03/05/1916	05/05/1916
War Diary	Laventie	06/05/1916	09/05/1916
War Diary	Fauquisart	09/05/1916	13/05/1916
War Diary	Laventie	14/05/1916	17/05/1916
War Diary	Robermetz	18/05/1916	25/05/1916
War Diary		20/05/1916	20/05/1916
War Diary	Pont Du Hem	26/05/1916	29/05/1916
War Diary	Moated Grange Laventie	29/05/1916	02/06/1916
War Diary	Pont Du Hem	03/06/1916	08/06/1916
War Diary	Moated Grange Laventie	08/06/1916	11/06/1916
War Diary	La Gorgue	11/06/1916	12/06/1916
War Diary	Gonneham	12/06/1916	14/06/1916
War Diary	Cauchy-A-La Tour	15/06/1916	15/06/1916
War Diary	Marquay	15/06/1916	25/06/1916
War Diary	Rougefay	26/06/1916	26/06/1916
War Diary	Bernaville	27/06/1916	30/06/1916
Heading	13th Battn. The Royal Welch Fusiliers. July 1916		
Heading	War Diary For July 1916 13 Batt. R.W.F. Vol 8		

War Diary	Herissart	01/07/1916	01/07/1916
War Diary	Lealvillers	02/07/1916	03/07/1916
War Diary	Treux Mametz	04/07/1916	04/07/1916
War Diary	Mametz	05/07/1916	11/07/1916
War Diary	Minden Post	12/07/1916	12/07/1916
War Diary	Yaucourt	13/07/1916	13/07/1916
War Diary	Brucamps.	14/07/1916	14/07/1916
War Diary	Authie.	15/07/1916	16/07/1916
War Diary	Lt Leger	17/07/1916	17/07/1916
War Diary	Area T.16 (near Coigneux)	18/07/1916	23/07/1916
War Diary	Baumont Hamel (Sector)	24/07/1916	27/07/1916
War Diary	Baumont-Hamel	27/07/1916	28/07/1916
War Diary	Bus-Les-Artois	28/07/1916	28/07/1916
War Diary	Sarton	29/08/1916	29/08/1916
War Diary	Doullens	30/07/1916	30/07/1916
War Diary	Hopoutre Houtkerque	31/07/1916	31/07/1916
Heading	13 Battn. RWF War Diary For August 1916 Vol 9		
War Diary	Houtkerque	01/08/1916	02/08/1916
War Diary	Poperinghe (area) Camp. K.	02/08/1916	05/08/1916
War Diary	Camp L	06/08/1916	20/08/1916
War Diary	Chateau Des Trois Tours.	21/08/1916	31/08/1916
Heading	War Diary 13th Battalion R.W.F. For September 1916. Vol 10		
War Diary	Chateau Des Trois Tours	01/09/1916	01/09/1916
War Diary	Right Sub-Sector	02/09/1916	06/09/1916
War Diary	D. Camp A 30.a 9.1	07/09/1916	16/09/1916
War Diary	Chateau Des Trois Tours.	17/09/1916	21/09/1916
War Diary	Right Sub-Sector	22/09/1916	23/09/1916
Miscellaneous	Report On Raid Carried Out By A Party Of The 13th Battalion Royal Welsh Fusiliers On The Night 19/20th September 1916	20/09/1916	20/09/1916
Miscellaneous	Report On Raid Carried Out By 13th R.W.F. On Night 28th/29th Septr. 1916	29/09/1916	29/09/1916
War Diary	Right Sub Sector	24/09/1916	27/09/1916
War Diary	Chateau Des Trois Tours.	28/09/1916	30/09/1916
Heading	War Diary 13th. Battalion Royal Welsh Fusiliers. October 1916 Vol 11		
War Diary	Chateau Des Trois Tours	01/10/1916	01/10/1916
War Diary	B.28.a.6.1 1/2. Canal Bank. C.19.c.4.4	02/10/1916	06/10/1916
War Diary	Chateau	07/10/1916	07/10/1916
War Diary	B 28.a.b.1 1/2. Canal Banks E & W.	08/10/1916	12/10/1916
War Diary	Right Sub-Section Left Sector	12/10/1916	15/10/1916
War Diary	D Camp A.30	16/10/1916	23/10/1916
War Diary	Chateau Des Trois Tours	24/10/1916	25/10/1916
Miscellaneous	Report On Raid Carried Out By 13th Royal Welsh Fusiliers On Night 12th/13th October 1916	13/10/1916	13/10/1916
War Diary	Canal Bank C 19.c. 4.4	26/10/1916	29/10/1916
War Diary	Canal Bank Right Sub-Section. C. 19.c. 4.4	30/10/1916	30/10/1916
War Diary	Chateau Des Trois Tours.	31/10/1916	31/10/1916
Heading	War Diary 13th Battalion Royal Welsh Fusiliers November 1916 Vol 12		
War Diary		01/11/1916	30/11/1916
Heading	13th. Battn Royal Welsh Fusiliers War Diary For December 1916 Vol 13		
War Diary	In The Field	01/12/1916	31/12/1916

Heading	War Diary For January 1917 13th Battn. Royal Welsh Fusiliers Vol 14		
War Diary	In The Field	01/01/1917	31/01/1917
Heading	War Diary 13th Battn. RWF. February 1917 Vol 15		
War Diary	In The Field	01/02/1917	28/02/1917
Heading	13th Battn. Royal Welsh Fusiliers War Diary For March 1917 Vol 16		
War Diary	In The Field	01/03/1917	31/03/1917
Heading	13th Battn. Royal Welsh Fusiliers War Diary For April 1917 Vol 17		
War Diary	In The Field	01/04/1917	30/04/1917
Heading	13th Royal Welsh Fusiliers War Diary For May 1917 Vol 18		
War Diary	In The Field	01/05/1917	31/05/1917
Heading	13th Batt. Royal Welsh Fusiliers War Diary For June 1917 Vol 19		
War Diary	In The Field	01/06/1917	18/06/1917
War Diary	In The Field Nile Sub Section.	19/06/1917	24/06/1917
War Diary	In The Field [Nile] Right Sub Section	25/06/1917	30/06/1917
Heading	13th Bn Royal Welsh Fusiliers War Diary July 1917 Vol. 20		
War Diary	In The Field	01/07/1917	31/07/1917
Heading	13th Battn Royal Welsh Fusiliers War Diary August-1917 Vol 21		
War Diary	In The Field	01/08/1917	31/08/1917
Heading	13th Batt. Royal Welsh Fusiliers War Diary For September 1917 Vol 22		
War Diary	In The Field	01/09/1917	30/09/1917
Heading	13th Batt. Royal Welsh Fusiliers War Diary For October 1917 Vol 23		
War Diary	In The Field	11/10/1917	31/10/1917
Heading	13th Batt. Royal Welsh Fusiliers War Diary For November 1917 Vol 24		
War Diary	In The Field	01/11/1917	30/11/1917
Heading	13th Batt. Royal Welsh Fusiliers War Diary For December 1917 Vol 25		
War Diary	In The Field	01/12/1917	31/12/1917
Heading	13th Batt. Royal Welsh Fusiliers War Diary For January 1918. Vol 26		
War Diary	In The Field	01/01/1918	31/01/1918
Heading	War Diary 13th Battalion Royal Welch Fusrs. February 1918 Vol 27		
War Diary	In The Field	01/02/1918	28/02/1918
Heading	13th Battn Royal Welsh Fusiliers War Diary For March-1918 Vol 28		
War Diary		01/03/1918	27/03/1918
War Diary	In The Field	28/03/1918	31/03/1918
Heading	13th Battn. The Royal Welch Fusiliers. April 1918		
Heading	13th Battalion R W Fus. War Diary April 1918 Vol 29		
War Diary	In The Field	01/04/1918	30/04/1918
Heading	War Diary For The Month Of May 1918 13 R.W.F. Vol. 30		
War Diary	Field	01/05/1918	31/05/1918
Heading	13th Batt. Royal Welsh Fusiliers. War Diary For June 1918 Vol 31		
War Diary	Field	01/06/1918	09/06/1918

War Diary	Field	08/06/1918	21/06/1918
War Diary		19/06/1918	19/06/1918
War Diary	Field	21/06/1918	30/06/1918
Heading	13th Batt. Royal Welsh Fusiliers War Diary For July 1918 Vol 32		
War Diary	In The Field	01/07/1918	31/07/1918
Heading	13th Batt Royal Welsh Fusiliers War Diary For August 1918 Vol 33		
War Diary	In The Field	01/08/1918	31/08/1918
Heading	War Diary For September 1918 13th Batt. Royal Welsh Fusiliers Vol 34		
War Diary	In The Field	01/09/1918	30/09/1918
Heading	13th R.W.F. War Diary For October 1918 Vol 35		
War Diary	Heudecourt	01/10/1918	03/10/1918
War Diary	Peiziere-Epehy	04/10/1918	04/10/1918
War Diary	Doleful Post	05/10/1918	05/10/1918
War Diary	Le Catalet Area	06/10/1918	06/10/1918
War Diary	Mortho Wood	07/10/1918	08/10/1918
War Diary	Bertry	16/10/1918	18/10/1918
War Diary	Montay	19/10/1918	20/10/1918
War Diary		08/10/1918	08/10/1918
War Diary	Mallincourt	09/10/1918	12/10/1918
War Diary	Bertry	13/10/1918	15/10/1918
War Diary	Montay	20/10/1918	21/10/1918
War Diary	Bertry	22/10/1918	22/10/1918
War Diary	Forrest	23/10/1918	23/10/1918
War Diary	Montay	20/10/1918	20/10/1918
War Diary	Forest	24/10/1918	25/10/1918
War Diary	Poix Du Nord	26/10/1918	31/10/1918
Heading	13th R.W.F. War Diary For November 1918 Vol 36		
War Diary	Poix du Nord (Bivonacs)	01/11/1918	04/11/1918
War Diary	Engle Fontaine	04/11/1918	05/11/1918
War Diary	Locquignol	06/11/1918	06/11/1918
War Diary	Ribaumet	07/11/1918	07/11/1918
War Diary	Dourlers	08/11/1918	08/11/1918
War Diary	Wattignies	09/11/1918	23/11/1918
War Diary	Sarbaras	24/11/1918	30/11/1918
Heading	13th R.W.F. War Diary For December 1918 Vol 37		
War Diary	Sarbaras	01/12/1918	27/12/1918
War Diary	Poix De Nord	28/12/1918	28/12/1918
War Diary	Inchy	29/12/1918	29/12/1918
War Diary	Franvillers	30/12/1918	31/12/1918
Heading	13th Battn Royal Welsh Fusiliers War Diary For January 1919 Vol 38		
War Diary	Franvillers	01/01/1919	31/01/1919
War Diary	Franvillers Nr. Amiens	01/02/1919	28/02/1919
War Diary	Franvillers	01/03/1919	17/03/1919
War Diary	Blangy Tronville (Nr Combined)	18/03/1919	20/03/1919
War Diary	Blangy Tronville	21/03/1919	30/04/1919

WO/95/2555/1

13 Battalion Royal
Welsh Fusiliers

38TH DIVISION

113TH INFY BDE

13TH BN ROY.WELSH FUS.

DEC 1915 - APR 1919

[illegible] 38th Edition [illegible]

[illegible]

12
1809

ORIGINAL

Instructions regarding War Diaries and Intelligence Summaries are contained in F. S. Regs., Part II. and the Staff Manual respectively. Title pages will be prepared in manuscript.

WAR DIARY
or
~~INTELLIGENCE SUMMARY.~~
(Erase heading not required.)

Army Form C. 2118.

13th Batt Royal Welch Fusiliers

Place	Date 1915	Hour	Summary of Events and Information	Remarks and references to Appendices
WINCHESTER	Dec 1	5-30	The Battalion Paraded at WINNALL DOWN CAMP WINCHESTER and marched off en Route for SOUTHAMPTON DOCKS for Embarkation. Throughout the Journey there was a heavy downpour of rain which added additional weight to the Clothes & Equipment carried by the men. The Distance covered was 15 miles which made a total of some 80 miles covered by the men in full marching order in new Boots, during the week. The Battalion arrived intact five minutes before the appointed hour (12 noon) owing to the rough state of weather the Battalion was split up and embarked on four Vessels. Exceptionally rough crossing	OH
HAVRE	Dec 2		Arrived at HAVRE between 7 and 8 am, disembarked and marched to Rest Camp. Paraded at 5 oclock marched in heavy rain to the Station and Entrained at 6 Pm.	OH
	Dec 3		Halted at ABBEVILLE 8.55 Am for 25 minutes, owing to an accident on the line the train did not reach ST OMER until 7 Pm instead of 2 Pm. Rough Plan of billeting area was handed to us here. The train proceeded to BLANDECQVES at which place the Battalion detrained and marched	
ECQUES	to		to ECQUES arriving there about 9-30 Men Billeted in Barns.	OH
	Dec 11		x During this time Improvements to Billets, Training in Musketry, Bombing Bayonet fighting &c was carried out. The Inhabitants of ECQUES proved very hospitable to the men providing them with hot Water facilities for cooking &c and were favourably impressed by the behaviour ho Claims for damage.	OH

2353 Wt. W2544/1454 700,000 5/15 D. D. & L. A.D.S.S./Forms/C. 2118.

ORIGINAL

Instructions regarding War Diaries and Intelligence Summaries are contained in F. S. Regs., Part II. and the Staff Manual respectively. Title pages will be prepared in manuscript.

WAR DIARY
or
~~INTELLIGENCE SUMMARY.~~
(Erase heading not required.)

Army Form C. 2118.

13th Batt Royal [illegible]

Place	Date	Hour	Summary of Events and Information	Remarks and references to Appendices
[illegible]	[illegible]		[illegible] with the exception of the transport [illegible] to LAVENTIE [illegible] for instruction in the trenches. [illegible] B Co. [illegible] 1st Welsh Guards [illegible] Guards [illegible]	
[illegible]			[illegible]	
			[illegible]	

8353 Wt. W2544/1454 700,000 5/15 D. D. & L. A.D.S.S. [illegible]

ORIGINAL

Instructions regarding War Diaries and Intelligence Summaries are contained in F. S. Regs., Part II. and the Staff Manual respectively. Title pages will be prepared in manuscript.

WAR DIARY
or
INTELLIGENCE SUMMARY.
(Erase heading not required.)

Army Form C. 2118.

13th Battalion Royal Welch Fusiliers.

Place	Date	Hour	Summary of Events and Information	Remarks and references to Appendices
POINT du HEM	Dec 14 cont		A coy going into Trenches with 2nd Irish Guards and B coy with 3rd Grenadier Guards going into Trenches	OLH
"	Dec 16		Battalions exchanged duties	OLH
	Dec 18		C & D coys came out of Trenches with Battalions to which they were attached. During the time of this attachment the only casualties which occurred were Pte Samuel Jones D coy. Shot through the head. Pte Solomon Thomas C coy. Shot through the hand. During this attachment each Platoon was attached to a different Company of the Guards Battalions	OLH
LE SART	Dec 19	1-30	Battalion was conveyed in the busses bringing 15th Batt R.W.F. to new Billeting Area at LE SART	OLH
	20		Head Quarters 113th Brigade arrived	OLH

2353 Wt. W2544/1454 700,000 5/15 D. D. & L. A.D.S.S./Forms/C. 2118

ORIGINAL

Instructions regarding War Diaries and Intelligence Summaries are contained in F. S. Regs., Part II. and the Staff Manual respectively. Title pages will be prepared in manuscript.

WAR DIARY
or
INTELLIGENCE SUMMARY.
(Erase heading not required.)

Army Form C. 2118.

13th Batt Royal Welch Fusiliers

Place	Date	Hour	Summary of Events and Information	Remarks and references to Appendices
[illegible] Sept	21		[illegible]	
			[illegible] General Holiday	
			[illegible]	

4353 Wt W2544/1454 700,000 5/15 D. D. & L. A.D.S.S./Forms/C 2118

13th R. W. Fus:
Vol 2
Jan 16

38th Div

2.B.
7 sheets

Instructions regarding War Diaries and Intelligence Summaries are contained in F. S. Regs., Part II and the Staff Manual respectively. Title pages will be prepared in manuscript.

WAR DIARY
or
~~INTELLIGENCE SUMMARY~~.
(Erase heading not required.)

Army Form C. 2118.

13th Batt Royal Welch Fusl

Place	Date	Hour	Summary of Events and Information	Remarks and references to Appendices
LE [illegible]T	Aug 1st		Training Conference of Batt [illegible] Commanders at Brigade Office	
	2nd		Church Parade. All officers attend a Lecture by the XI Corps Commander General R C Haking	
	3rd		Col [illegible] Fraser (CO) Capt [illegible] (Adjt) and Four Company Commanders ([illegible] A Co, Major [illegible] B Co, Capt [illegible] C Co, Capt [illegible] D Co) and [illegible] proceeded by motor Bus to LE TOURET and inspected trenches [illegible] Rue du Bois [illegible] proceeded to HQ [illegible] and went around [illegible] Trenches [illegible] [illegible]	
	4		[illegible]	

4553 Wt W2544/1454 700,000 5/15 D. D. & L. A.D.S.S./Forms/C 2118

Instructions regarding War Diaries and Intelligence Summaries are contained in F. S. Regs., Part II. and the Staff Manual respectively. Title pages will be prepared in manuscript.

WAR DIARY
or
INTELLIGENCE SUMMARY.
(Erase heading not required.)

Army Form C. 2118.

13 Batt Royal Welch Fusl.

Place	Date	Hour	Summary of Events and Information	Remarks and references to Appendices
LE SART. to KINGS ROAD	Jany 5th		The Battalion marched down to Brigade Reserve Billets at X 11 + 17. Ref Sheet 36 A. We left LE SART at 8-30 in the morning and arrived at 11-30 Am. Very few men fell out & those that did all rejoined. We took over Billets from 7th South Lancs Regt.	OV7
	6th		In evening after dark the Battalion proceed to relieve 7th Batt. North Lancs in the Trenches. The front occupied by the Battalion being from QUINQUE RUE CROSSING. Ref. Secret map 36 SW3. to FARM CORNER. A coy on Right Front & B coy on Left Front – C coy Right Support in TUBE STATION and D coy in Battalion Reserve in RUE DES BERCEAUX. The relief was completed by 7-30 Pm. there were no Casualties	OV7
	Jan 7th		An enemy's patrol was seen during the night and dispersed on being fired at. During the day it was quiet. at 10.30 pm A patrol under Lt Vaughan went out from our left company. but were unable to reach enemy's wire owing to being fired at.	OV7
	Jan 8th		During the morning enemy's Artillery fired a number of Shells on Prince's Road. In the afternoon three men from 'C' Coy were hit by pieces of bursting shell no one hurt seriously. 'C' Coy relieved 'A Coy & 'D' Coy relieved 'B' in the firing line. Patrol under Lt Wynne Edwards. went out at 12.20 a.m (midnight) and returned at 1.20 a.m. They discovered a working party of the enemy. which was fired upon by our machine guns.	OV7

Army Form C. 2118.

WAR DIARY
or
INTELLIGENCE SUMMARY.
(Erase heading not required.)

B Batt Royal [illegible]

Instructions regarding War Diaries and Intelligence Summaries are contained in F. S. Regs., Part II. and the Staff Manual respectively. Title pages will be prepared in manuscript.

Place	Date	Hour	Summary of Events and Information	Remarks and references to Appendices
	Jan 9th		Fairly quiet during the day but at night two men were shot by flanking shots.	
			Patrol went out to investigate Old German Communication Trench [illegible] for about 150 x [illegible] but saw no [illegible] of the enemy	
	Jan 10th		Our Art'y [illegible] during the day but enemy did not reply to the same extent. [illegible] suffered [illegible] but did no damage. After dark the Batt was relieved [illegible] Batt R.W.F. [illegible] Road in ~~Batt~~ Brigade Reserve. During this tour of duty a great [illegible] work was done in improving the first line trenches, support trenches and Keeps. The [illegible] [illegible] the parts joined up, good deal of drainage was done, [illegible] [illegible]	
	Jan 11th 12th 13th		in BRIGADE RESERVE in KINGS Rd. Parties employed in improving the drainage [illegible] [illegible] the road [illegible] passable. Working parties supplied for work in front sector.	
	Jan 14th		Moved into DIVISIONAL RESERVE in billets N of LE TOURET, relieving 6th Batt WILTS regiment. Poor billets & accommodation very [illegible].	
	Jan 15th		Brigadier inspected [illegible] billets.	
	Jan 16th		Company [illegible] Batt Training	
	Jan 17th		[illegible] Draft of twenty [illegible] arrived. The [illegible]	
			[illegible] at LESTREM	
			Staff [illegible] under Major Gen'l [illegible] G.O.C. 19th Division [illegible] of routes to be followed for [illegible] of Battalion [illegible]	

2353 Wt W2544/1454 700,000 5/15 D. D. & L. A.D.S.S./Forms/C 2118.

Instructions regarding War Diaries and Intelligence Summaries are contained in F. S. Regs., Part II. and the Staff Manual respectively. Title pages will be prepared in manuscript.

WAR DIARY
or
INTELLIGENCE SUMMARY.
(Erase heading not required.)

Army Form C. 2118.

13th Bn Royal Welch Fusl

Place	Date	Hour	Summary of Events and Information	Remarks and references to Appendices
FORWARD area	Jan 19th		Compy in Battalion Training. 130 at Follies Entertainment at LESTREM	
	Jan 20th		Usual training. Serious bombing accident occurred; a grenade exploded prematurely while a party of 'B' Coy were practicing grenade throwing. Three men killed and Lt W D Parry and five men injured. Capt Lawrence RAMC, M.O for Battn. arrived on the scene of the accident and skilfully attended the wounded with great promptitude, and sent them to Field Ambulance with great despatch.	OJJ
"	Jan 21st		Compy and Battn classes of Instruction continued.	OJJ
"	Jan 22nd.		" " " " " " " .	OJJ
"	Jan 23rd.		Relieved 4th KING'S LIVERPOOL Regt from QUINQUE CROSSING to RUE DE CAILLOUX and 6th WILTS Regt from latter point to FARM CORNER. A and B Coy in front line. 'C' Coy right support at TUBE STATION finding garrisons for DEAD COW and CHOCOLATE POST. D Coy left support at TEETOTAL CORNER and NEW BREASTWORK.	OJJ
"	Jan 24th		In morning enemy shelled new barrier at QUINQUE CROSSING and during day both front line and support trenches. One 77mm shell ~~passed~~ hit dugout in which C.S.M Sharpe 'B' Coy was sitting. The fuse cap remained in dug out but did no damage. During the night three patrols under 2/Lt Wynne Edwards. Fairchild & Jenkins went out to investigate ground in front of the line	OJJ
"	Jan 25th		Usual Hostile Shelling. Three casualties in front line trenches. Company relief.	OJJ
"	Jan 26th		Our artillery bombarded briskly but very little retaliation. Our snipers accounted for two enemy snipers. who were observed from newly constructed snipers posts. They had been seen to go to their positions at dawn and one was shot as he was crawling back at 4.15pm the other while in the act of firing	OJJ

$353 Wt. W2544/1454 700,000 5/15 D. D. & L. A.D.S.S./Forms/C. 2118.

Instructions regarding War Diaries and Intelligence Summaries are contained in F. S. Regs., Part II. and the Staff Manual respectively. Title pages will be prepared in manuscript.

WAR DIARY
or
INTELLIGENCE SUMMARY.
(Erase heading not required.)

Army Form C. 2118.

13th Bn Royal Welch Fusiliers

Place	Date	Hour	Summary of Events and Information	Remarks and references to Appendices
[illegible]	26th		A four patrols went out to investigate state of German wire. An unusual number of Very lights & star shells were fired from 10.15 (midnight) to 1 a.m.	
	27th		Kaiser's Birthday. A good deal of Artillery activity on both sides. Our Arty [illegible] after dark. Battn was relieved by 14th Battn R.W.F. Relief [illegible] 7.35 pm. [illegible] KRIG RISERVE [illegible] KINGS ROAD.	
	28th / 29th		[illegible] of [illegible] working parties [illegible] from the trenches. Enemy shelled [illegible] GMS [illegible] damage to bath house and [illegible] bathing parties. One officer & 2 [illegible] WILTS [illegible] attached to Battalion for instruction.	
			During the period [illegible] 23rd to 29th [illegible] a great amount of work was done to improve shelters [illegible] so that [illegible] [illegible] nearly isolated posts. The [illegible] [illegible]	
			[illegible]	

8353 Wt. W2541/1454 700,000 5/15 D. D. & L. A.D.S.S./Forms/C. 2118

Instructions regarding War Diaries and Intelligence Summaries are contained in F. S. Regs., Part II. and the Staff Manual respectively. Title pages will be prepared in manuscript.

WAR DIARY
or
INTELLIGENCE SUMMARY.
(*Erase heading not required.*)

Army Form C. 2118.

Place	Date	Hour	Summary of Events and Information	Remarks and references to Appendices
FORWARD AREA	Feby 1st		In Trenches. Our artillery shelled FME. DU BOIS from 12 noon until 2 Pm at S.16. c 6.6 for the purpose of cutting wire. Enemy retaliated on front line Breastwork with about 40 77MM shells doing some damage to Parapet N of the CORNER (Post) Officers Patrol under LT JENKINS went out from FARM CORNER at 1 Am to investigate damage done to enemys wire Progress was very difficult owing to thin ice on ditches and patrol was unable to reach wire owing to strong enemy patrol being encountered	OA
	2		Enemy shelled Princes Road. C coy relieved A coy in front trenches (RIGHT) and D coy relieved B coy in front trenches (LEFT) A & B Coys forming supports at NEW BREASTWORK & TEETOTAL CORNER respectively. Two Enemy working parties located & dispersed with Machine Gun fire	OA
	3		Tube STATION PRINCESS ROAD & FARM CORNER shelled by Enemy. At 11-40 Pm a Party under LT WYNNE EDWARDS went out to lie in wait for enemy in old German Communication Trench running from S 22. c 58. which trench had been reported as being used by enemy as a listening Post and for Sniping Purposes. The Party remained out until 2 Am but no enemy was observed	OA
	4		Front-line trenches, TUBE STATION TEETOTAL CORNER & CHOCLATE BREASTWORK again shelled by enemy otherwise quiet. RELIEVED by 14th RWF & went into BRIGADE Reserve billets in KINGS ROAD relief completed 7-10 PM. During this tour of duty a great amount of work has been done in the improvement of front line trenches both as regards protection & accommodation. The majority of the Posts have now been joined up and it is possible to get from one	OA

Army Form C. 2118.

WAR DIARY
or
INTELLIGENCE SUMMARY.
(Erase heading not required.)

Instructions regarding War Diaries and Intelligence Summaries are contained in F. S. Regs., Part II. and the Staff Manual respectively. Title pages will be prepared in manuscript.

Place	Date	Hour	Summary of Events and Information	Remarks and references to Appendices
	4 contd		end of the line to the other with comparative safety. Parados have been erected in dangerous places. A great number of Fire Steps Tunnel Boards &c have been put in and the protecting wire has been greatly improved. The same remarks apply to work done at TUBESTATION, DEADCOW, CHADBURY and other support posts.	
	5th		In Brigade Reserve Billets. Large Parties provided for work in front section and also for improvement in Billeting Area	
	6th		ditto ditto ditto	
	7th		ditto ditto ditto	
	8.		Relieved by the 8th [illegible] Regiment 114th Brigade in KINGS ROAD and we took over Billets [illegible] them in [illegible] Reserve at [illegible] LOBES [illegible] over 15 Rooms, the [illegible] of which were [illegible] by [illegible]	
	9		Reserve. We [illegible] at Divisional H.Q. [illegible] 6-20 AM a Test [illegible] "[illegible]" – Companies were ordered to "Stand To" [illegible] and [illegible] ammunition [illegible] were issued [illegible]	
	10		We gave a Concert at Divisional H.Q.	

#353 Wt. W2544/1454 700,000 5/15 D. D. & L. A.D.S.S./Forms/C. 2118

Instructions regarding War Diaries and Intelligence Summaries are contained in F. S. Regs., Part II. and the Staff Manual respectively. Title pages will be prepared in manuscript.

WAR DIARY
or
INTELLIGENCE SUMMARY.
(Erase heading not required.)

Army Form C. 2118.

Place	Date	Hour	Summary of Events and Information	Remarks and references to Appendices
LOCON	11		Divisional Reserve. The Commanding Officer 2nd in Command and Officers commanding Companies reconnoitred lines of advance to front line trenches	OB
"	12		Divisional Reserve The Battalion gave a Concert in the MILL LOCON	OB
"	13		Divisional Reserve Sunday Church Parade The C.O. 2nd in Command Four officers commanding Companies, Machine Gun Officer, & Bombing Officer visited new line to be taken over by Battalion on 17/2/16 at GIVENCHY	OB
"	14		Divisional Reserve.	OB
"	15		Divisional Reserve. The Adjutant - QMR. Signalling Officer and one Officer per Company visited new line at GIVENCHY to be taken over by us.	OB
"	16		Divisional Reserve	

2353 Wt. W2544/1454 700,000 5/15 D. D. & L. A.D.S.S./Forms/C. 2118.

Army Form C. 2118.

WAR DIARY
or
INTELLIGENCE SUMMARY.
(Erase heading not required.)

Instructions regarding War Diaries and Intelligence Summaries are contained in F. S. Regs., Part II. and the Staff Manual respectively. Title pages will be prepared in manuscript.

Place	Date	Hour	Summary of Events and Information	Remarks and references to Appendices

4353 Wt. W2544/1454 700,000 5/15 D. D. & L. A.D.S.S./Forms/C. 2118

Instructions regarding War Diaries and Intelligence Summaries are contained in F. S. Regs., Part II. and the Staff Manual respectively. Title pages will be prepared in manuscript.

WAR DIARY
or
INTELLIGENCE SUMMARY.
(*Erase heading not required.*)

Army Form C. 2118.

Place	Date	Hour	Summary of Events and Information	Remarks and references to Appendices
			After explosion of mine our men opened rapid fire on enemy's front line & did exceedingly well under trying circumstances – We were relieved by 14th Battn R W F and relief completed at 9.15 p m. We relieved 15th Battn in village line. Our snipers shot a German in sap head opposite our Sap F. During our tour in trenches communication was improved, parapet strengthened and stores for bombs & SAA built.	
Feb 22nd to Feb 25th			Occupied village line. Distribution being as follows 'B' & 'D' between WINDY CORNER & Wolferd entrance to ~~Trenches~~. 'C' at LE PLANTIN 'A' at Givenchy Keep, MOAT HOUSE & HARTS KEEP. During stay in village line working parties were provided for improvement of communication trenches. Heavy fall of snow.	
Feb 26th			Relieved 14th Battalion R.W.F Relief completed at 8.35 p.m Very quiet night & enemy's M.G was not so active at 'Standto'. Patrol went out from 'C' Sap at 9 p.m to endeavour to cross crater but were unable to do so owing to heavy nature of ground. Germans were heard singing well known English songs. Work of joining saps was continued & clearing snow & mud from trenches. Enemy working party observed from F2 Sap & fired upon. One man was killed & was seen to be carried in by his comrades half an hour later.	
Feb 27th			Heavy Arty bombardment during the day. A large percentage of "duds" were fired in the first stage but the shells improved later on. Enemy retaliated with HE but no damage was done. Enemy's patrol seen at A9 d 6.2½ and M.G fired upon them. Two of them were laid out & are now lying in NO MAN'S LAND. One of our aeroplanes flying very low drew a heavy M.G & rifle fire from ENEMY. Our M.G seized the opportunity & traversed Enemy's parapet. Patrol under Lt Wynne Edwards went out on left of line to ascertain damage done to Enemy's wire. They found working party on enemy's wire & on their return turned our M G on them	

3353 Wt. W2544/1454 700,000 5/15 D. D. & L. A.D.S.S./Forms/C. 2118.

Army Form, C. 2118.

Instructions regarding War Diaries and Intelligence Summaries are contained in F. S. Regs., Part II. and the Staff Manual respectively. Title pages will be prepared in manuscript.

WAR DIARY
or
INTELLIGENCE SUMMARY.
(Erase heading not required.)

Place	Date	Hour	Summary of Events and Information	Remarks and references to Appendices
			we fired a large no of rifle grenades but did not draw much retaliation	
Feb 27			Very quiet day until our Art'y commenced operations when enemy replied with A.K. but no damage done. Rum jars & grenades were fired at left of our line immediately retaliated with Art'y fire. A patrol under 2/Lt R M Wynne Edwards went out to find damage done to enemy's wire. When about 40 yds from enemy's wire they encountered enemy's patrol they threw a bomb at them but damage was not known. A patrol under 2/Lt Phillips went out to find 5 dead Germans. Owing to darkness they were unable to find bodies & it is believed they had been taken in by their comrades. Our aeroplane flying low drew heavy M.G. rifle fire from enemy, it seemed that he was very anxious to keep him away. Work of clearing trenches was continued as the thaw had made the communication trenches very wet & dirty. [illegible]	
Feb 29			[illegible]	

2353 Wt. W2544/1454 700,000 5/15 D. D. & L. A.D.S.S./Forms/C. 2118.

38

13 RW Fus

Vol 4

March 1916

4.B.
6 sheets

Instructions regarding War Diaries and Intelligence Summaries are contained in F. S. Regs., Part II. and the Staff Manual respectively. Title pages will be prepared in manuscript.

WAR DIARY

or

INTELLIGENCE SUMMARY.

(Erase heading not required.)

Army Form C. 2118.

Place	Date	Hour	Summary of Events and Information	Remarks and references to Appendices
[illegible]			[illegible]	

W353 Wt. W2544/1454 700,000 5/15 D. D. & L. A.D.S.S./Forms/C. 2118

Army Form C. 2118.

Instructions regarding War Diaries and Intelligence Summaries are contained in F. S. Regs., Part II. and the Staff Manual respectively. Title pages will be prepared in manuscript.

WAR DIARY
or
INTELLIGENCE SUMMARY.
(Erase heading not required.)

Place	Date	Hour	Summary of Events and Information	Remarks and references to Appendices
Trenches in Givenchy.	8th		Enemy sent over several 77 mm HE few falling near 'C' Coy H.Q. Retaliation soon stopped their firing. Heavy bombardment on our right in direction of Hohenzollern. One of enemy shot by sniper just before 'stand to' in the Evening. Work of strengthening parapet, draining & laying trench boards continued under great disadvantage as the trench was in a very bad state after the snow. We were relieved by 10th Welsh Regt from 52 Street to 57 Street, Gunners Siding & MARIE REDOUBT. Relief Complete at 7.45 p.m	OH
			Relieved by 15 Welsh Regt from 57 Street to Hamilton Rd. Relief Complete 10 p.m	OH
Les Choquaux	9th		Battalion back for 8 days rest. Col Howe went on leave.	OH
	16th		During this period Men fired on the range. Advanced instruction in bombing was given, Physical Drill & bayonet fighting. All men were bathed & given change of Clothing.	OH
			Large fatigue parties for wiring near LE TOURET were found every day.	
	15		New Officers (Barrett, Evans, Hunt, Edwards, Hughes) arrive.	OH
	16th		Left Les Choquaux for village line at Festubert. Here we relieved 14th Bn RWF. Relief complete at 9.30 p.m.	OH
Festubert.	17th		Village line Festubert. Very quiet, except for occasional shelling at Brewery Corner & Festubert. Weather Glorious. Men employed on Wiring during the nights. Huns dropped three 4.2 in Orchard behind H.Q.	OH
	18		Village line. Few Shrapnel burst near H.Q. The usual daily shelling of Brewery Corner & Festubert.	OH
	19		Village line	OH
	20		Huns shelled Battery at Estaminet Corner. Very slight damage done. Battalion relieved 14th Battn RWF in trenches. Relief complete 9.30 p.m	OH

a353 Wt. W2544/1454 700,000 5/15 D. D. & L. A.D.S.S./Forms/C. 2118.

Army Form C. 2118.

Instructions regarding War Diaries and Intelligence Summaries are contained in F. S. Regs., Part II. and the Staff Manual respectively. Title pages will be prepared in manuscript.

WAR DIARY
or
INTELLIGENCE SUMMARY.
(Erase heading not required.)

7

Place	Date	Hour	Summary of Events and Information	Remarks and references to Appendices

2353 Wt. W2544/1454 700,000 5/15 D. D. & L. A.D.S.S./Forms/C 2118.

Army Form C. 2118.

Instructions regarding War Diaries and Intelligence Summaries are contained in F. S. Regs., Part II. and the Staff Manual respectively. Title pages will be prepared in manuscript.

WAR DIARY
or
INTELLIGENCE SUMMARY.

(Erase heading not required.)

Place	Date	Hour	Summary of Events and Information	Remarks and references to Appendices
Front Line Trenches	28th		Relieved 14th Battalion R.W.F. Very dark stormy night but enemy inactive. Nothing of any importance happened throughout the night. 'C' Coy occupied right group of Islands and D Coy left group	O.A.
	29th		Very quiet day except for little shelling which did no damage. Our snipers were very aggressive and claim two victims. Battalion did much hardwork on islands, O.B.L. and Cover Trenches.	O.A.
	30th		Enemy was a little more active with Arty fire but no damage was done. Hardly a rifle shot was fired throughout the day except by our snipers. We sent out a patrol to examine enemy's wire. They got quite near & by aid of Very lights could see it quite clearly. Inter Coys relief. 8 Enemy observation balloons were out during the day	O.A.
	31st		Aerial activity during the morning and Artillery was a little more active dropping shells in front of RICHMOND TRENCH, in Old German Line and Rope Keep. This increase in activity was due to clear day for observing Arty fire. During the night there was more than usual rifle fire all along our front. Work of joining islands strengthening parapets & wiring was gone on with.	O.A.

8353 Wt. W2544/1454 700,000 5/15 D. D. & L. A.D.S.S./Forms/C. 2118.

XXXVIII

Army Form C. 2118.

Vol 5

WAR DIARY or INTELLIGENCE SUMMARY.

(Erase heading not required.)

Instructions regarding War Diaries and Intelligence Summaries are contained in F. S. Regs., Part II. and the Staff Manual respectively. Title pages will be prepared in manuscript.

13th Batt Royal Welch Fusiliers

Place	Date	Hour	Summary of Events and Information	Remarks and references to Appendices
Festubert	1/4/16		Relieved by 10th Welsh Regt and proceeded to billets at Les Choquaux in Divisional reserve. Lt Williams of 20th RWF joined this Battn and Lt O.S. Jenkins who was sick went into hospital.	
Les Choquaux	2/4/16		Major Campbell returned off leave. } During this period Battn was in divisional reserve at Les Choquaux. Work done – Training; specialists under specialist officers all companies under their coy commanders	
"	4/4/16		Transport inspected by GOC XI corps and a congratulatory report received as to its efficiency	
"	7/4/16		Major Bell & Lt Aubertin returned from leave	
Givenchy Lez-la-Bassée	9/4/16		We relieved 15th RWF in the Village line	
		2.20am	Enemy exploded a mine opposite the center coy of the left Battn – a few casualties occured including 3 of our men.	
"	10/4/16		Large fatigue parties were found for work on saps and communication trenches. Cleared up trenches in all the keeps & rebuilt many portions. Establishment of ammunition and bomb stores adjusted. Wire in front of Village line S considerably strengthened. Captain R Hardwick sent to hospital with measels.	
"	11/4/16		Enemy shelled vicinity of Pont Fixe bridge with 77. Several shells failed to explode and little damage was done.	
"	12/4/16		Lt Glyn Jones and 2/Lt Swain proceeded on leave. Cellars of Brewery were cleaned and made habitable. Work on the keeps continued.	
"	13/4/16		Relieved 14th RWF in front line trenches. Enemy were very quiet all day except for occasional bursts of MG fire. Enemy rifle grenades were replied to with interest. 30 yards of apron were put up in front of country str. and construction of a parapet joining left and center coy was commenced.	

6638

Instructions regarding War Diaries and Intelligence Summaries are contained in F. S. Regs., Part II. and the Staff Manual respectively. Title pages will be prepared in manuscript.

WAR DIARY, or INTELLIGENCE SUMMARY.

(Erase heading not required.)

Army Form C. 2118.

13th Bn ROYAL WELCH FUS.

Place	Date	Hour	Summary of Events and Information	Remarks and references to Appendices
Givenchy Les-la-Bassée	14/4/16		Enemy very quiet. Continued building parapet between center and right coy.	
	15/4/16	11.30pm	Relieved by 13th Sussex Regt. We proceeded to Les Choquaux and billeted there.	
Les Choquaux	16/4/16		Marched to Estaires + billeted in the town for the night. Major Campbell returned from leave.	
Laventie	17/4/16		Relieved 10th Batt. Worcester Regt at Winchester House.	
"	18/4/16		The enemy shelled at intervals during the day. HE and shrapnel. The top end of Winchester trench and all the posts appear to be well registered by the enemy. Lt Glyn Jones + 2/Lt Swain returned from leave.	
"	19/4/16		Enemy's artillery active throughout the day. Winchester trench and all the posts were again shelled. A heavy shell, certainly not less than an 8" fell in the front line. About 50 yards of apron wire were erected. During the whole tour which lasted from 10pm 17/4/16 to 10pm 20/4/16 the enemy artillery were very active + it was evident that the top end of Winchester ~~tr~~ trench and all the posts were well registered by the enemy. The enemy appeared to be working actively in the craters. Much work was done in the way of rebuilding and draining.	OJ
	20/4/16		We were relieved by the 14th RWF. Batt marched to ~~to Robermetz~~ Pont du Hem and billeted there.	6648

#353 Wt. W2544/1454 700,000 5/15 D. D. & L. A.D.S.S./Forms/C. 2118.

Army Form C. 2118.

WAR DIARY
or
INTELLIGENCE SUMMARY.
(Erase heading not required.)

Instructions regarding War Diaries and Intelligence Summaries are contained in F. S. Regs., Part II. and the Staff Manual respectively. Title pages will be prepared in manuscript.

Place	Date	Hour	Summary of Events and Information	Remarks and references to Appendices
Pont du Hem	21/4/16		Nil } in Brigade support	
	22/4/16		Lt G Edwards joined the Battn } in Brigade support	
	23/4/16		2/Lt B Hardwick granted special leave } in Brigade support	
	24/4/16		Marched into Robermetz & billeted there.	
Robermetz			~~Up to this day~~ From 24/4/16 to this day 27/4/16 Battn in Divn reserve. Work done – training. Bombers, Snipers, Signallers etc under specialist officers and coys under Coy commanders	
	25/4/16 to 29/4/16		Training as above	
	30/4/16		Marched to Laventie and took over billets from 17th Bn [illegible]	
Laventie	1/5/16		Took over line from 16th Welsh Regiment in the FAUQUISSART Section. Relief completed at 10 pm. [illegible] in front line also [illegible] posts ie ELGIN, FAUQUISSART, [illegible]	
	2/5/16		Early in the morning Capt Gordon Jones was slightly wounded by a bomb explosion. Artillery fairly active during the day shelling Fauquissart post and the church [illegible]	

6616/4B

2353 Wt. W2544/1454 700,000 5/15 D. D. & L. A.D.S.S./Forms/C. 2118.

Instructions regarding War Diaries and Intelligence Summaries are contained in F. S. Regs., Part II. and the Staff Manual respectively. Title pages will be prepared in manuscript.

WAR DIARY (38) or INTELLIGENCE SUMMARY.

(Erase heading not required.)

13 R Welsh 2 Vol 6

Army Form C. 2118.

Place	Date	Hour	Summary of Events and Information	Remarks and references to Appendices
FAUQUISART	3/5/16		Enemy artillery was fairly active during the day. FAUQUISART CHURCH was shelled for ½ hour about midday.	
	"	11.25pm	Two strong german patrols were encountered just outside our wire at M24 b 5.1 and M24 b 1.3½ (Bde trench map area J). They retired & heavy fire was opened on our line from an old trench in No man's land & from the enemy's line assisted by a search light. We replied with rapid rifle fire and MG fire. The enemy patrol appeared to be wearing caps similar to ours. The two patrols mentioned above were connected by smaller parties covering in all 200 to 300 yds of front. Enemy MG's were very active till 6am this morning. Work on the parapet, damaged by enemy shells yesterday, was continued. ~~Capt Lees & Capt Hardwich proceeded on leave.~~	
	4/5/16		Enemy very quiet during the day our rifle grenades drawing very little retaliation. Our howitzers fired on an enemy front line dugout during the morning. The ~~rest~~ result was disappointing as 10 of the rounds were duds. After stand to the enemy lapsed into unusual calmness & very few very lights were seen.	
		11pm	A good deal of shouting over to our line	
			Two patrols went out on our right but nothing of importance was noticed. Capt Lees and Capt Hardwich proceeded on leave.	
	5/5/16		The enemy's artillery was very active all day our parapet being hit on four occasions. One round destroyed a MG emplacement and the gun. Our artillery retaliation was feeble and most of the few rounds sent over were duds.	666p SB

2353 Wt. W2544/1454 700,000 5/15 D. D. & L. A.D.S.S./Forms/C. 2118.

6B 6 sheets

Instructions regarding War Diaries and Intelligence Summaries are contained in F. S. Regs., Part II. and the Staff Manual respectively. Title pages will be prepared in manuscript.

WAR DIARY
or
INTELLIGENCE SUMMARY.
(Erase heading not required.)

Army Form C. 2118.

Place	Date	Hour	Summary of Events and Information	Remarks and references to Appendices
FAUQUISSART	5/5/16		The enemy sent over two lots of about 15 Rifle grenades: badly directed. We retaliated with about 40 Rifle grenades which appeared to be well placed and stopped the enemy's fire. A sandbag wall was noticed in a building at N19 a 7½.2 (Bde trench map Sheet J) which looks as if it might be used as a night MG emplacement.	
		9.35 pm	We were relieved by 14th RDF relief commenced at 8 pm completed at 9.35 pm The Battn moved into LAVENTIE and took over billets from 14th RDF	
LAVENTIE	6/5/16 to 9/5/16		RE fatigues & musketry. During this period Battn was in Brigade Reserve. [illegible] joined the Battn.	
FAUQUISSART	9/5/16		Took over from 14th RDF. Relief completed 9.35 pm. A [illegible] the completion of the [illegible] could not be [illegible]	[illegible]
	11/5/16		Enemy's artillery active all day. ROTTEN ROW communication trench and FAUQUISSART KEEP were heavily shelled. Our retaliation was prompt and effective.	
		9.15 pm to 9.25 pm	Lights were observed falling over AUBERS also in a SW direction. These lights appeared to be dropped from an ~~areoplain~~ aeroplane. It was intended to carry out the raid [illegible] so a small party was sent ahead to examine the gaps in enemy's wire. Half way there they encountered a party of [illegible] germans. ~~[illegible]~~ Our party being outnumbered	

2353 Wt. W2541/1454 700,000 5/15 D. D. & L. A.D.S.S./Forms/C. 2118.

Instructions regarding War Diaries and Intelligence Summaries are contained in F. S. Regs., Part II. and the Staff Manual respectively. Title pages will be prepared in manuscript.

WAR DIARY
or
INTELLIGENCE SUMMARY.
(*Erase heading not required.*)

Army Form C. 2118.

Place	Date	Hour	Summary of Events and Information	Remarks and references to Appendices
			~~bombed the enemy and retired.~~ ~~retired~~. A strong patrol under Lt Wynne-Edwards + 2/Lt HUGHES went out to search the spot but could find no dead or wounded. They moved on towards the enemy's wire and found that he was very vigilant and appeared to be standing to. He was also sending up numerous very lights. The party returned + we opened fire on his line. Much work was done in repairing parapet damaged by enemy shelling yesterday and repair of communication trenches.	
	11/5/16		An enemy patrol was encountered and driven off with bombs This occurred opposite the right coy. Enemy patrols were also encountered and driven off opposite the left coy.	
	12/5/16		Enemy shelled our front line at 8 am the shells dropping near a trench mortar. They damaged the parapet at this point.	
		9.30/pm	A patrol went out to investigate a trench in no mans land under Lt Thomas + Hughes. Nothing was observed so the order to retire was given while the two officers a cpl and one man covered their retreat. A party of over 30 Germans advanced on the covering party after the patrol had reached our trench. The Germans were held up and eventually repelled thanks to the efficiency of the MILLES HAND GRENADE A patrol went out to examine a ruin in no mans land at N 19 a 0.7 and found a dead German.	6688

2353 Wt. W2544/1454 700,000 5/15 D. D. & L. A.D.S.S./Forms/C. 2118.

Army Form C. 2118.

WAR DIARY
or
INTELLIGENCE SUMMARY.
(Erase heading not required.)

Instructions regarding War Diaries and Intelligence Summaries are contained in F. S. Regs., Part II. and the Staff Manual respectively. Title pages will be prepared in manuscript.

Place	Date	Hour	Summary of Events and Information	Remarks and references to Appendices
			A patrol went out under Lt J Evans & encountered an enemy patrol which [illegible] successfully driven off. A break was [illegible] in the enemy's parapet opposite [illegible] 1½ to the right of [illegible] there [illegible] & between this and the break is a [illegible] Evidently the break is a sally port.	
		[illegible]	A [illegible] mine was exploded well to our right. Lt V Jones [illegible] on leave	
	13/5/16		During the afternoon our artillery knocked out an MG emplacement at N13 [illegible] 6½. This emplacement appeared to enfilade the [illegible]. [illegible] with [illegible] on RUE TILLELOY. Hostile MGs were rather more active than usual at stand to in the evening and morning. We were relieved by the 14th RWF. Relief complete at 10 p.m. We marched into LAVENTIE and took over billets from the 14th RWF.	
LAVENTIE	14/5/16 to 17/5/16		Battn in Brigade reserve at LAVENTIE. 2/Lt EVANS joined the battn on 16th inst	
	17/5/16		We were relieved by 15th Welsh Regt and marched into ROBERMETZ where we took over billets from 13th Welsh Regt. Capt LEES and [illegible] returned off leave	

2353 Wt. W2544/1454 700,000 5/15 D. D. & L. A.D.S.S./Forms/C. 2118.

Instructions regarding War Diaries and Intelligence Summaries are contained in F. S. Regs., Part II. and the Staff Manual respectively. Title pages will be prepared in manuscript.

WAR DIARY
or
INTELLIGENCE SUMMARY.
(Erase heading not required.)

Army Form C. 2118.

Place	Date	Hour	Summary of Events and Information	Remarks and references to Appendices
ROBERMETZ	18/5/16 to 25/5/16		Coy training, and training of specialists under specialist officers. Occasionally, R.E. fatigues. Battallion at rest. Relieved in billets by the 17th R.W.F., and marched into PONT-du-HEM taking over billets from 10th S.W.B.	
	20/5/16		LE SART rifle range, competition shoot in conjunction with the 16th R.W.F.	
PONT du HEM.	26/5/16 to 29/5/16		Battalion in Brigade Reserve, Lt. 7 R.G. Thomas and Lt. Ellis proceeded on leave.	
MOATED GRANGE LAVENTIE	29/5/16		We relieved the 14th R.W.F. Relief complete at 9.50 p.m.	
		12 p.m	Two patrols from 14th R.W.F., proceeded from M.24 d ½.3½.	
	30/5/16	2-30 a.m.	During stand to the enemy fired 50 and 60 rifle grenades at the junction of ERITH trench and front line. During the afternoon the enemy sent over a large number of rifle grenades on our left company, who retaliated in a like manner.	
		7-0 p.m.	Enemy commenced a heavy bombardment, on our front and support lines in the right sub-section, travelling ~~from~~	6 Vol

WAR DIARY
or
INTELLIGENCE SUMMARY.
(Erase heading not required.)

Army Form C. 2118.

Instructions regarding War Diaries and Intelligence Summaries are contained in F. S. Regs., Part II. and the Staff Manual respectively. Title pages will be prepared in manuscript.

Place	Date	Hour	Summary of Events and Information	Remarks and references to Appendices
MOATED GRANGE			from South northwards, and chiefly concentrated about the BIRD CAGE, by artillery, accompanied by heavy T.M and rifle	
LAVENTIE	30/5/16		grenades. Our artillery retaliating.	
		7.45pm	Telephone communication between Battalion Headquarters and the Companies in the first line was cut.	
		8.5pm	Visual signalling with centre company established	
		8.20pm 9.50pm 8.35pm	Telephonic communication re-established with centre, right and left companies respectively.	
		9.40pm	Bombardment gradually died down, but M.G fire increased. No attempt by the enemy to leave their trenches.	
	31/5/16		Enemy very inactive during the day, and less than usual M.G fire at night.	

2353 Wt. W2544/1454 700,000 5/15 D. D. & L. A.D.S.S./Forms/C 2118.

13 Welsh
Army Form C. 2118.
Fus
Vol 7

Instructions regarding War Diaries and Intelligence Summaries are contained in F. S. Regs., Part II. and the Staff Manual respectively. Title pages will be prepared in manuscript.

XXXVIII

WAR DIARY
or
INTELLIGENCE SUMMARY.
(*Erase heading not required.*)

June

Place	Date	Hour	Summary of Events and Information	Remarks and references to Appendices
MOATED GRANGE LAVENTIE	1/6/16		We registered with N.P. Grenades on German trench about M 30. c 5.9. also with Stokes Gun on the line from M 30. a.4.1. to M. 30 a 3.3.	
		8.	Listening Post opposite CENTRE Coy reported no enemy patrols seen or work proceeding in the craters.	
			Officers patrol went out from M 29 b 9.3. in S.E direction, and surprised a party of the enemy in "NO MAN'S LAND" who retired quickly to their front trench; This patrol reported that a great deal of work was in progress in the enemies trench	OA
			Another patrol went out from M 30 a.3.7. and proceeded to the enemies wire cutting same at M 30. a. 6½. 5.	
	2/6/16	3.10 am 4-0 am	Our Artillery dispersed working parties at points M.30 c.5. 8 and M 30 c 5.9 respectively.	OA
			Our Snipers claim victims at M 29. d 3.0	
		3. 2 p.m	Our medium T.M.B fired about 8 bombs on the enemy's front line. Retaliation was drawn, the enemy replying with salvoes of Shrapnel & LHV on the BIRDCAGE and right company.	
			Our rifle-grenade battery fired about 90 grenades at a point which had been previously registered. Heavy	OA

6771 SB
7.B 6 sheets

5353 Wt. W2544/1454 700,000 5/15 D. D. & L. A.D.S.S./Forms/C. 2118.

WAR DIARY
or
INTELLIGENCE SUMMARY.
(Erase heading not required.)

Army Form C. 2118.

Instructions regarding War Diaries and Intelligence Summaries are contained in F. S. Regs., Part II. and the Staff Manual respectively. Title pages will be prepared in manuscript.

Place	Date	Hour	Summary of Events and Information	Remarks and references to Appendices
[illegible]			Shrapnel was [illegible] over the left platoon (right company [illegible] N. of [illegible]) causing casualties. Our artillery promptly replied, and eventually the hostile shelling ceased at 4.25 p.m.	
		[illegible]	Relief [illegible] by the 14th R.W.F. completed 10.30 p.m. [illegible] returned to the Battalion, 2nd [illegible] proceeded on leave.	
Po[illegible]			Battalion in reserve. R.E. fatigues and company drill [illegible]	
	7/6/16 8/6/16		During the night 2nd Vaughan and large fatigue party in conjunction with fatigue party from the 16th R.W.F. under command of R.E. Officer, commenced cutting trench. The 13th RWF party (from about point M.29 b 10.3½) in a [illegible] direction, and the 16th R.W.F party (from about point M.29 d 10.7) in a northerly direction [illegible] to [illegible] our front line.	
			[illegible] completed at 10.25 p.m. [illegible]	
			[illegible] M.30 a 9.5 [illegible]	

6/4[illegible]

Instructions regarding War Diaries and Intelligence Summaries are contained in F. S. Regs., Part II. and the Staff Manual respectively. Title pages will be prepared in manuscript.

WAR DIARY
or
INTELLIGENCE SUMMARY.
(Erase heading not required.)

Army Form C. 2118.

Place	Date	Hour	Summary of Events and Information	Remarks and references to Appendices
MOATED GRANGE LAVENTIE	9/6/16		at 11 0 a.m. the enemy's artillery fired 5 rounds shrapnel to the rear of our right Coy. the last round bursting over the front line. No reply from our guns. Continuation of new trench from M.30.a½.3½. to M.30.c.0.7. and single apron of wire erected along the whole length.	OJJ
	10/6/16 11/6/16		at 1 0 a.m. enemy's artillery fired 8 rounds H.E. on RUE-du-BAC QUEROT, near cross roads, M.22.b.8½.5. Between 1-0 a.m and 1-40 a.m. artillery on both sides fairly active about NEUF CHAPELLE. Our artillery fired at intervals throughout the day, the enemy made no attempt at retaliation. Two officers observed wearing blue uniform, white braid on shoulder straps, round peaked caps with red band and white braiding round rim.	OJJ
LA GORGUE	11/6/16		Relieved by the 2/6th Gloucester Regt relief complete at 10-50 p.m. Battalion marched to billets at LA-GORGUE, all men in billets at 1-45 a.m.	
	12/6/16		Battalion commenced to march to allotted area for Divisional rest and training. Battalion left LA GORGUE at 12-5 noon via LESTREM, L'EPINETTE, PARADIS, PACANT and HINGES to the GONNEHEM area & billets	OJJ
GONNEHAM	13/6/16		GONNEHEM rested for the day, Short route marches by company's	OJJ

6746

$353 Wt. W2544/1454 700,000 5/15 D. D. & L. A.D.S.S./Forms/C. 2118.

Army Form C. 2118.

Instructions regarding War Diaries and Intelligence Summaries are contained in F. S. Regs., Part II. and the Staff Manual respectively. Title pages will be prepared in manuscript.

WAR DIARY
or
INTELLIGENCE SUMMARY.
(Erase heading not required.)

Place	Date	Hour	Summary of Events and Information	Remarks and references to Appendices
[illegible]	[illegible]		[illegible] from [illegible] at [illegible] a.m. [illegible] LOZ[illegible] and marched to [illegible] where they billeted for the night.	[illegible]
[illegible]			[illegible] at [illegible] a.m. via FLORINGHEM, PERNES, [illegible] and [illegible] (MARA[illegible]) arriving at 12-15 noon.	[illegible]
			Companies [illegible] at the Divisional Training Ground.	
			U 2 [illegible] 36 B	
	[illegible]		[illegible] by the General Officer Commanding-in-Chief [illegible] the Military Medal to [illegible] [illegible] for [illegible] conduct in the field during the [illegible] 23-24 [illegible] [illegible] 1916. [illegible]	
	[illegible]		[illegible] Company [illegible]	
			Extract from London Gazette dated [illegible] Temporary Captain [illegible] 7 April 1915 [illegible] Nov 1915 [illegible] to be [illegible] 1 Apr 1916 [illegible]	
			[illegible] (Capt [illegible]) [illegible] to [illegible]	[illegible]

6914

W 3353 Wt W.2541/1454 700,000 5/15 D. D. & L. A.D.S.S./Forms/C 2118.

Instructions regarding War Diaries and Intelligence Summaries are contained in F. S. Regs., Part II. and the Staff Manual respectively. Title pages will be prepared in manuscript.

WAR DIARY
or
INTELLIGENCE SUMMARY.
(Erase heading not required.)

Army Form C. 2118.

Place	Date	Hour	Summary of Events and Information	Remarks and references to Appendices
MARQUAY	19/6/16		Lt Oswald Jenkins, "C" Coy of this Battalion, rejoined Unit.	OH
	21/6/1916 to 23/6/1916		Battalion schemes of attack, assault & defence on allotted Divisional area.	OH
	24/6/1916		Brigade scheme of attack on enemy's 2nd line system, assault & consolidation, Divisional area.	OH
	25/6/1916		Divisional Exercise, consolidating 1st German system, attack and assault on 2nd German system and Tactical Points in 3rd German system.	OH
ROUGEFAY	26/6/1916		Battalion marched at 5 p.m. from MARQUAY to billetting area at ROUGEFAY — via:- TERNAS, BUNEVILLE, NUNCQ, LIGNY-SUR-CANCHE and VACQUERIE-LE-BOUCQ to ROUGEFAY.	OH
BERNAVILLE	27/6/16		Battalion marched from ROUGEFAY at 8.15 p.m. to billetting area at BERNAVILLE, via:- BOFFLES, VILLERS-L'HOPITAL, FROHEN-LE-GRAND and LE MEILLARD to BERNAVILLE.	OH
			The G.O.C. in Chief has awarded the following rewards to this Battalion for gallant conduct in the field during the bombardment of our front line on May 30th 1916. Military Medal to No. 17491 L/Sgt. D. H. Rees, No. 17263 L/Cpl. T. H. Davies and No. 16706 Pte C. Edwards.	OH

6/76

Instructions regarding War Diaries and Intelligence Summaries are contained in F. S. Regs., Part II. and the Staff Manual respectively. Title pages will be prepared in manuscript.

WAR DIARY
or
INTELLIGENCE SUMMARY.
(Erase heading not required.)

Army Form C. 2118.

Place	Date	Hour	Summary of Events and Information	Remarks and references to Appendices
BERNAVILLE	29/5/16		Battalion practised orders to "Stand to". Company inspection.	
	30/5/16		Medical inspection, Arms & musketry drill, Defence of village	
	31/5/16		Moved off from BERNAVILLE at 4-30 p.m. via FIENVILLERS, CANDAS, Fme DU ROSEL and LE VAL DE MAISON to HERISSART.	

#553 Wt W2544/1454 700,000 5/15 D. D. & L. A.D.S.S./Forms/C. 2118.

113th Inf.Bde.
38th Div.

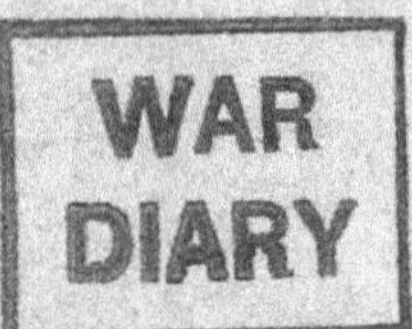

13th BATTN. THE ROYAL WELCH FUSILIERS.

J U L Y

1 9 1 6

Instructions regarding War Diaries and Intelligence Summaries are contained in F. S. Regs., Part II. and the Staff Manual respectively. Title pages will be prepared in manuscript.

13/38

WAR DIARY
or
INTELLIGENCE SUMMARY.
(Erase heading not required.)

Army Form C. 2118.

Vol 8

Place	Date	Hour	Summary of Events and Information	Remarks and references to Appendices
			WAR DIARY FOR JULY 1916 13 BATT. R.W.F.	

T2134. Wt. W708–776. 500000. 4/15. Sir J. C. & S.

13th Royal Welsh Fusiliers

WAR DIARY
or
INTELLIGENCE SUMMARY.
(Erase heading not required.)

Instructions regarding War Diaries and Intelligence Summaries are contained in F. S. Regs., Part II. and the Staff Manual respectively. Title pages will be prepared in manuscript.

Army Form C. 2118.

Place	Date	Hour	Summary of Events and Information	Remarks and references to Appendices
HÉRISSART	1/7/16	10.20 P.M	The Battalion marched from HÉRISSART into billets at LEALVILLERS, via TOUTENCOURT.	RWC
LEALVILLERS	2/7/16		Company inspection musketry and arm drill. The following Officers reported and were duly posted to the Battalion:- (1) 2nd Lt H.E.R. Ford (11th (Res) GLOSTERS, attached) (2) 2nd Lt E. L. Davies (3) 2nd Lt J. E. Price, (4) 2nd Lt R.W. Thomas (5) 2nd Lt Hugh Jones (6) 2nd Lt R. Scott Vaughton (7) 2Lt David Thomas, and (8) 2nd Lt H Bryn Jones.	RWC
	3/7/16		2nd Lt J. M. Owen (transferred from 16th R.W.F.) reported, and was duly posted to the Battalion.	RWC
		8.40pm	The Battalion marched from LEALVILLERS at 8.40p.m via VARENNES, WARLOY-BAILLON, BAIZIEUX, RIBEMONT-SUR-ANCRE, and MERICOURT-L'ABBE to TREUX.	
TREUX	4/VII/16.		Company inspection, musketry and arm drill	
MAMETZ	5/VII/16.		The Battalion marched from TREUX at 12 noon to MAMETZ via - VILLE-SOUS-CORBIE, MÉAULTE, BÉCORDEL, BÉCOURT & FRICOURT	RWC
			Relieved the 22ND MANCHESTERS in FRITZ TRENCH and DANTZIC ALLEY	
		7.30pm	Relief complete	
			FRITZ TRENCH and DANTZIC ALLEY occasionally shelled during the evening with shrapnel and	
			MAMETZ shelled during the night 5-6/VII/16/. with H.H.E. (5.9)	
	6/VII/16.		Heavy bombardment by our Artillery with shrapnel and H. E. on QUADRANGLE ALLEY, QUADRANGLE SUPPORT TRENCH, WOOD SUPPORT TRENCH, MAMETZ WOOD, ACID DROP COPSE and 2ND LINE SYSTEM.	RWC

#353 Wt. W2544/1454 700,000 5/15 D. D. & L. A.D.S.S./Forms/C. 2118.

Instructions regarding War Diaries and Intelligence Summaries are contained in F. S. Regs., Part II. and the Staff Manual respectively. Title pages will be prepared in manuscript.

WAR DIARY
or
INTELLIGENCE SUMMARY.
(Erase heading not required.)

Army Form C. 2118.

Place	Date	Hour	Summary of Events and Information	Remarks and references to Appendices
MAMETZ	6/7/16		Enemy retaliated on MAMETZ village at intervals with H.E. (5.9)	
		[illegible]	B and C Coys moved forward to front line, B Company occupying WHITE TRENCH from [illegible] to [illegible] ALLEY, and C Company occupying CATERPILLAR WOOD.	
			Bombardment by our Artillery continued during the night 6/7/16 – 7/7/16.	
	7/7/16	[illegible]	[illegible] made an attack on [illegible]	
		[illegible]	A [illegible] attack [illegible] of the [illegible] on the West side and [illegible] of the 38th Welsh Division [illegible] East side of MAMETZ WOOD was made, the [illegible] being to capture the Wood. The attack was preceded by a heavy bombardment by our Artillery and during the attack a barrage was [illegible] attacking troops. [illegible] the Cardiff [illegible] Wood [illegible]	Officers killed in action
			[illegible] Bazentin Wood and [illegible] Wood. The attack [illegible] from [illegible] Trench [illegible]	
	[illegible]	[illegible]	[illegible] Wood, [illegible] Wood and [illegible] Alley [illegible] — During the night [illegible] by [illegible] West end of [illegible] of a strong [illegible]	2/Lt [illegible] wounded
			[illegible] Wood relieved by [illegible] Welsh [illegible] and [illegible]	

Army Form C. 2118.

WAR DIARY
or
INTELLIGENCE SUMMARY.
(Erase heading not required.)

Instructions regarding War Diaries and Intelligence Summaries are contained in F. S. Regs., Part II. and the Staff Manual respectively. Title pages will be prepared in manuscript.

Place	Date	Hour	Summary of Events and Information	Remarks and references to Appendices
MAMETZ	9/VII/16.	P.M. 12.30. – 2 P.M.	MAMETZ and ALBERT to CARNOY ROAD heavily shelled by the enemy (chiefly 5.9.) who succeeded in hitting one of our artillery ammunition stores. — Weather fine.	2/LT. H.T. Edwards taken to hospital suffering from Shell-Shock. RWC
		2.30 P.M.	Two companies were withdrawn from DANTZIC ALLEY and bivouaced on ground near HALT south of CEMETERY [MAMETZ] — 2/Lt. H.T. Edwards went out of action owing to shell shock.	
	10/VII/16.	A.M. 4.45	38TH. Division attacked MAMETZ WOOD.	
			Disposition of forces – Right flank:– From Centre side of wood to extreme East side of Wood, 114TH. Brigade.	
			Left flank:– From Centre side to West side of Wood, 113TH. Brigade.	
			Formation:– 113TH. Brigade in 8 lines at 100 yards per battalion, the 16TH R.W.F. 1ST. line being formed up North of WHITE TRENCH.	RWC
			Capt. E.W. Lawrence R.A.M.C. ~~and~~ 2/Lt. A.S.H. Barrett and Lieut. H. Vivian Jones, were killed in action while Capts. L. S. Ayer and F.R.G. Thomas were wounded.	
	11/VII/16.	7 am.	Three patrols were sent forward to reconnoitre ground up to the railway line, on their returning the line advanced our right being in touch with the 16TH. Welsh. Patrols were sent out to extreme edge of Wood.	2/Lt. J. Prichard was also wounded in action RWC
		12 Noon	Battalion relieved on this line by 16TH. R.W.F. and moved back to the original line. S of [illegible] in	
		3.30 pm	X24B. where at 3.30 pm the C.O., Major Bell and Adjt: were wounded by one of our own shells – Capt. Hardwick took command.	
		5.37 pm.	Battalion moved forward to X roads at Y.	
		7.25 pm.	Under orders Battalion andvanced and formed line on R of 14. R.W.F. with 3 Coys. and 1 Coy: on L of 14 R.W.F. forming new front line.	
		10.0 pm.	Orders received from Brig-Gen. Evans to evacuate new line and to take over 2nd line held by 11. S.W.B. on R. of CENTRAL RIDE with 3 Coys. & 1 Coy on L of CENTRAL RIDE.	
MINDEN POST	12/VII/16.	1.0 am.	Battalion relieved in this line by 12TH Northumberland Fusiliers (21ST Div) and bivouaced near MINDEN POST.	
		5.30 pm.	Battalion marched to the HALTE at MEAULTE and entrained for LONGPRE and thence marched to billets at YAUCOURT. — 2/LT. H.R. Ford rejoined for duty.	RWC

8353 Wt. W2544/1454 700,000 5/15 D. D. & L. A.D.S.S./Forms/C. 2118.

Army Form C. 2118.

Instructions regarding War Diaries and Intelligence Summaries are contained in F. S. Regs., Part II. and the Staff Manual respectively. Title pages will be prepared in manuscript.

WAR DIARY
or
INTELLIGENCE SUMMARY.
(Erase heading not required.)

Place	Date	Hour	Summary of Events and Information	Remarks and references to Appendices
YAUCOURT.	[illegible]	[illegible]	Batt. arrived at YAUCOURT.	
		[illegible]	[illegible] inspection.	
[illegible]	[illegible]	[illegible]	Batt. marched from YAUCOURT into billet at [illegible].	
[illegible]	[illegible]	[illegible]	Batt. moved to AUTHIE by [illegible]	
	[illegible]	[illegible]	[illegible]	
[illegible]	[illegible]	[illegible]	[illegible] (Troops) – [illegible] 3RD [illegible]	
			[illegible]	
[illegible]	[illegible]	[illegible]	[illegible]	
	[illegible]	[illegible]	[illegible]	2 [illegible] fatigue party [illegible]
			[illegible] 2 p.m. to [illegible]	
	23/[illegible]	10 a.m.	Church parade. – Fatigue parties (R.E.) – The following officers reported and were duly posted to the Batalion – (1) 2/Lt. [illegible] (2) 2/Lt. [illegible] (3) 2/Lt. [illegible] & 2/Lt. [illegible]. [(Res) GLOSTERS attached.]	
[illegible]	24/[illegible]	[illegible]	Battalion took over [illegible] [BAUMONT HAMEL sector] from the 9TH. R. FUSILIERS. Relief complete at [illegible] p.m. Enemy [illegible] relief shelled 5TH AVENUE Com. Trench causing four casualties ([illegible] R.T.)	
		[illegible]	Front line [illegible] with large T.Ms – Retaliation by our Artillery.	
		[illegible]	Hostile [illegible] (H.E.) At about [illegible] p.m. enemy working party observed: our Artillery shelled the point Q 5 [illegible] [illegible]	
	[illegible]	[illegible]	Relief of [illegible] by [illegible] complete. Hostile Artillery during the day causing damage to BURROW, [illegible] BUSTER and [illegible] trenches. Night quiet. [illegible]	
		[illegible]	2/Lt. [illegible] Edwards [illegible] reconnoitred the REDAN RIDGE and returned at [illegible] p.m. reporting [illegible] working parties. [illegible] communication trench damaged by our Art. fire.	
	27 [illegible]	[illegible]	[illegible] Lewis Gunners opened fire on enemy's working party (wiring) several of the enemy were seen to fall. Enemy's wiring very thick along [illegible] of [illegible] line – gaps in places.	

8353 Wt. W2544/1454 700,000 5/15 D. D. & L. A.D.S.S./Forms/C. 2118.

Army Form C. 2118.

Instructions regarding War Diaries and Intelligence Summaries are contained in F. S. Regs., Part II. and the Staff Manual respectively. Title pages will be prepared in manuscript.

WAR DIARY
or
INTELLIGENCE SUMMARY.
(Erase heading not required.)

Place	Date	Hour	Summary of Events and Information	Remarks and references to Appendices
BEAUMONT-HAMEL.	27/vii/16	2.30pm	Two hostile planes over our "lines" were fired upon by our anti-aircraft guns. – later	
		6.30pm	6 enemy planes over German lines were fired upon by our anti-aircraft guns, while two of	
		7 pm	our planes were seen flying under hostile squadron, and gradually mounting. Our two planes patrolled until dusk.	RWC
	28/vii/16		Occasional hostile shelling; our Art. shelled BEAUMONT-HAMEL.	
BUS-LES-ARTOIS		11.50am.	Relief of Battalion by 17TH. S.L.I. complete – Batt: moved out of the "line" and marched to BUS-LES-ARTOIS and occupied hutments there.	RWC
SARTON	29/vii/16	7.0am	Battalion marched from BUS to SARTON ~~where the~~ and billeted there. {Billets & Transport lines inspected by Brig. Gen.	
		9.30am	Bathing (vol.) parade, and inspection of rifles.	
DOULLENS	30/vii/16	2.15pm.	Batt. marched to Doullens where we entrained, leaving station at 6.15pm.	
HOPOUTRE	31/vii/16	2.0am.	Batt. detrained at HOPOUTRE near POPERINGHE and marched to billets at HOUTKERQUE	RWC
HOUTKERQUE		7.45am	via ABEELE and WATOU. (arrived at 7.45 am)	

R O Campbell Major

~~LIEUT. COL.~~
CMDG. 13th. BATT. ROYAL WELSH FUS.

2353 Wt. W2544/1454 700,000 5/15 D. D. & L. A.D.S.S./Forms/C. 2118.

Vol 9

13 BATT^N RWF

WAR DIARY FOR AUGUST 1916

Instructions regarding War Diaries and Intelligence Summaries are contained in F. S. Regs., Part II. and the Staff Manual respectively. Title pages will be prepared in manuscript.

WAR DIARY
or
INTELLIGENCE SUMMARY.

(Erase heading not required.)

Army Form C. 2118.

Place	Date	Hour	Summary of Events and Information	Remarks and references to Appendices
[illegible]	[illegible]	[illegible] am	Battalion parade [illegible] drill [illegible] [illegible] drill [illegible] [illegible]	
		[illegible] pm	2 [illegible] 30pm, bathing parade by Coys. and kit inspection	
	[illegible]	[illegible]	Coy. drill and [illegible] by platoons [illegible]	
POPERINGHE (area) Camp. K.		[illegible] pm	Battalion left [illegible] and moved into Camp K, about 2 000 yards W. of Poperinghe on [illegible]	
	3/[illegible]		Battalion parade 9.0 am [illegible] drill and arm drill [illegible] [illegible] and 2 [illegible] pm [illegible] [illegible] parade	
	[illegible]		Battalion parade 9.0 am Programme [illegible] as on 3/[illegible]	
	5/[illegible]		"	
Camp. L.	6/[illegible]		No parades, bathing by Coys. 8.0 am to 11.0 am. At 6.30 pm Battalion [illegible] moved [illegible] Camp [illegible] in same area.	Specialist parades for special training
	7/[illegible]		Arm drill and P.T. by platoons 6.30 am to 7.30 am 9.0 am to 12 noon and 2.0 pm to 4.30 pm under Coy: arrangement.	
	8/[illegible]		Arm drill and P.T. by platoons 6.30 am to 7.30 am 9.0 am to 12.45 pm. Battalion Route March.	
	[illegible]		" " " "	
	10/[illegible]		" " 9.0 am to 12 noon and 2.0 pm to 4.30 pm under Coy. arrangement	
	11/[illegible]		The Camp [L] was inspected by the Corps Commander [illegible]. Battalion parade, [illegible] [illegible] arrangement	
	12/[illegible]	[illegible] am	Battalion parade – marching order Battalion [illegible] route march [illegible] am to 11.0 am. Parade 2.45 pm to 4.30 pm by Coys.	
	13/[illegible]		Church Parade C of E – [illegible] Brigade, Church parade – [illegible] [illegible] Bns. [illegible] were present [illegible]	
		[illegible] am	[illegible] and Bayonet fighting [illegible] [illegible] was present.	
	14/[illegible]	[illegible] am	[illegible] with Brigade divided up [illegible] four classes – A, B, C & D classes. A class being the advanced class, all	
		[illegible]	[illegible] Officers of the Brigade [illegible] being in one class, similarly all Warrant Officers.	
		[illegible]	Same classes in Bayonet fighting – At 10.30 am Brigade paraded [illegible] General [illegible]	
			[illegible] to Officers Warrant Officers and Other Ranks of the [illegible] – Parades until 4.30 pm under Coy: arrangement.	
	15/[illegible]	6.45 am	Physical drill – 9.30 am to 10.15 am B.F. under same arrangements – 10.15 am to 12.30 pm 2.0 pm to 4.30 pm Coy. arrangement.	2/Lt. K. G. Edwards proceeded on special leave to Bangor.
	16/[illegible]	[illegible]	Programme of work as on 15/[illegible] – Bathing by Coys. 7.15 am to 11.30 am	
	17/[illegible]	6.45 [illegible]	P.T. [illegible] am to [illegible] am B.F. 10.15 am to 12.30 pm 2.0 pm to [illegible] pm under Coy. arrangement	
	18/[illegible]	[illegible] am	[illegible] [illegible] [illegible] to leaving men.	
	[illegible]	11.0 am	Church Parade.	
		9.45 pm	Battalion moved off from "L" Camp and marched to Poperinghe Station where the Batt: entrained at 11.0 pm.	

R O Campbell
LIEUT. COL.

5353 Wt. W2544/1454 700,000 5/15 D. D. & L. A.D.S.S./Forms/C. 2118.

Instructions regarding War Diaries and Intelligence Summaries are contained in F. S. Regs., Part II and the Staff Manual respectively. Title pages will be prepared in manuscript.

WAR DIARY
or
INTELLIGENCE SUMMARY.
(Erase heading not required.)

Army Form C. 2118.

Place	Date	Hour	Summary of Events and Information	Remarks and references to Appendices

2353 Wt. W2544/1454 700,000 5/15 D. D. & L. A.D.S.S./Forms/C. 2118.

Comdg. 13th Batt. Royal Welsh Fus.

Instructions regarding War Diaries and Intelligence Summaries are contained in F. S. Regs., Part II. and the Staff Manual respectively. Title pages will be prepared in manuscript.

Army Form C. 2118.

WAR DIARY
or
INTELLIGENCE SUMMARY.
(Erase heading not required.)

Place	Date	Hour	Summary of Events and Information	Remarks and references to Appendices
CHATEAU DES TROIS TOURS	30 Sept [illegible]	[illegible]	Very heavy rain throughout the day. Fatigue parties to R.E. Dumps and the Front line.	
	[illegible]		GAS ALERT OFF. Fatigue Parties carrying and unloading R.E. material.	

8353 Wt. W2544/1454 700,000 5/15 D. D. & L. A.D.S.S./Forms/C. 2118.

R. C. Campbell LIEUT. COL.
…13th BATT. ROYAL WELSH FUS.

Vol 10

– WAR DIARY –

13th BATTALION R.W.F.

FOR

SEPTEMBER 1916.

Instructions regarding War Diaries and Intelligence Summaries are contained in F. S. Regs., Part II. and the Staff Manual respectively. Title pages will be prepared in manuscript.

WAR DIARY
or
INTELLIGENCE SUMMARY.
(Erase heading not required.)

Army Form C. 2118.

Place	Date	Hour	Summary of Events and Information	Remarks and references to Appendices
CHATEAU DES TROIS TOURS	1/IX/16.	9.0p.m.	A German shell [5.9?] exploded outside the Signal Office killing 1 O.R. and wounding 4. Relief of C & D Coys. 14TH. R.W.F. by C & D Coys. of 13TH. R.W.F at 4.30p.m. Relief complete at 6.50p.m. Our Artillery experimented in wire cutting with a new type of shell result being the enemy retaliated with H.E. on our front line and on the CANAL BANK.	
		10.30pm	A & B Coys. relieved A & B Coys. of 14TH. R.W.F. A Coy. commencing at 10.30pm, and B at 11.0pm.	
RIGHT SUB-SECTOR.	2/IX/16.	12.15Am	Relief of A & B Coys. reported complete.	
		12.40am	An officer's patrol under 2/Lt. R.W. THOMAS went out from C.14.c.7.7. NO MAN'S LAND reported to be very muddy, shell holes water logged. Hammering was heard in enemy's lines at C.14.a.9.1. (approx.) A Lewis Gun fired in the direction mentioned – result unknown. Another patrol consisting of 1 Sgt. and 3 O.R. entered NO MAN'S LAND at C.13.b.1½.8., and moved off ½ right for 100 yds (approx) at which point they were able to hear the enemy working opposite C.14.a.2½.5. in their wire. On proceeding to the spot it was discovered	
		2.0am	that there was a large hostile patrol quite close to them. Our patrol then carefully retired and entered our trenches at 2.0am. – Lewis Guns fired in the direction of working parties and patrol.	
		2.30am	Our parapet was breached at C.14.a.8.4 for a distance of 8 yds. Covering Battery silenced hostile T.M. activity.	
		8pm.	Hostile T.M's were very active but our quick and plentiful retaliation silenced them in a very short time.	
		11.30pm	An officer's patrol under 2/Lt. HUGH JONES left our line at C.13.b.7.5½. and proceeded along ditch along wh. water flows into our line. A second patrol under 2/Lt. K.G. EDWARDS left our line at C.13.b.7½.7. to investigate suspected "listening post" in one of the shell holes. Though the patrol examined and remained at the spot for over an hour nothing could be seen or heard. "Two listening posts" at C.14.c.7.7. and C.14.c.5.10. in front of our wire had nothing to report.	
		11.15pm.	Gas Alarm sounded wh. later proved to be false. Origin believed to be on extreme right of SALIENT. Work was chiefly drainage and wiring. Thickening of parapet 2 right Coys.	

R.D. [illegible] Lt Col
Comm 13th R.W. Fus.

8353 Wt. W2544/1454 700,000 5/15 D. D. & L. A.D.S.S./Forms/C. 2118.

Army Form C. 2118.

Instructions regarding War Diaries and Intelligence Summaries are contained in F. S. Regs., Part II. and the Staff Manual respectively. Title pages will be prepared in manuscript.

WAR DIARY
or
INTELLIGENCE SUMMARY.

(Erase heading not required.)

Place	Date	Hour	Summary of Events and Information	Remarks and references to Appendices
RIGHT SUB-SECTOR.	3/12/16.	2.0am	Gas Alarm sounded which again proved to be false. Work done chiefly drainage and a deal of wire was put out at C13.b.9.2 and C14.c.9.6.	
	4/12/16	5.0pm.	No T.M. activity as previously experienced. Hostile shelling of CANAL BANK between BRIDGES 4 and 6. with 4.2s but no damage done.	
	5/12/16.	12.30AM	An officer's patrol went out from C13b.8.2½ and heard enemy working party behind his parapet, but could not locate it exactly. The grass in NO MAN'S LAND reported to about 2 feet high and numerous large shell holes to be seen. Patrol returned our line.	
		2.15AM	A second patrol went out from C14.c.5.9 and reported enemy working in his front line — sounds of patting sand-bags was heard. — About 36 yards of concertinas were put up at C13.b.7.9½, C14.c.9.2, C14.c.5.9, and C13.b.8.3. A Listening Post was established at C13.b.9.8½ but nothing was observed. The working party behind the enemy's line was located later as being near KRUPP FARM. — Judging from the hostile firing on our aeroplanes the enemy must have a considerable number of M.G.s and rifles in his line.	
	6/12/16.	[illegible] AM	A patrol left our line at about C13.b.7.6 and worked their way to within 6 yards of the enemy's wire. The wire was reported to be very strong. Many shell holes were encountered which had the appearance of having been occupied some time or other. Sounds of timber being pushed were heard.	
		12.50AM / 2.0AM	A second patrol went out from C13.b.7.2½ and reported No Man's Land to be very wet and the going difficult. A working party was heard in enemy's support line, and on patrols returning a Lewis gun was fired in the direction of the sounds. Probably some of the bullets took effect because loud shouts were heard.	
		8.15pm	The day was quiet. The 17th Bn. L.N.F. relieved 13th R.W.F. "A" Coy. 17th L.N.F. relieved "D" Coy. 13th R.W.F. along HUDDERSFIELD. "B" Coy. " " " " " "A" Coy. " " " along LANCASHIRE RAILWAY. "C" Coy. " " " " " "C" Coy. " " " along HUDDERSFIELD. "D" Coy. " " " " " "B" Coy. " " " along LANCASHIRE RAILWAY.	

[signature] Lt Col
13th Batt R W Fus

#353 Wt. W2544/1454 700,000 5/15 D. D. & L. A.D.S.S./Forms/C. 2118.

Army Form C. 2118.

Instructions regarding War Diaries and Intelligence Summaries are contained in F. S. Regs., Part II. and the Staff Manual respectively. Title pages will be prepared in manuscript.

WAR DIARY
or
INTELLIGENCE SUMMARY.
(Erase heading not required.)

Place	Date	Hour	Summary of Events and Information	Remarks and references to Appendices
D. CAMP. A 30 a 9.1.	7/IX/16		On relief A & D Coys. proceeded to D Camp via CHATEAU DES TROIS TOURS and B & C Coys. to the CANAL BANK EAST and closed up as near the bank as possible and waited there until the 16TH. Bn. WELCH REGT. had taken up SUPPORT LINE ON CANAL BANK. Orders were then issued to these two Coys. to proceed to D Camp. [A 30 A]	
		3.30 AM	The whole Bn. reported to have arrived at D Camp, and took over allotted hutments.	
			Battalion rested the remainder of the day.	
	8/IX/16.	5.0 AM.	The C.O. proceeded on SPECIAL LEAVE. Major LLOYD in command of the Battalion.	
		6.45 AM.	Battalion parade – PHYSICAL DRILL. (7.30 AM)	
		9.30 AM – 12.30 pm	Battalion paraded for Bayonet Fighting, & Coy. training.	
		2.0 pm	Parade until 3.0 pm. under Coy. arrangements.	
		3.0 pm	~~Four~~ officers – 1 ofr. from each Coy. – reported at 114TH. Bde. HQ for work on CANAL BANK DEFENCE SCHEME, but owing to absence of buses to convey fatigue parties from D Camp, work was cancelled.	
	9/IX/16.	6.45 AM	Physical Drill.	
		9.30 AM	Bayonet Fighting.	
		10.15 AM – 12.30 PM	Company and platoon drill.	
		2.0 PM – 4.30 PM	Parade under Company arrangements.	
	10/IX/16.	10.30 AM – 11.0 AM	Church parades Services for C of E and Welsh and English Nonconformists.	
	11/IX/16.	6.45 AM	Physical Drill	
		9.0 AM.	Bayonet Fighting	
		10.0 AM – 12.30 pm	Battalion Drill and training under Company arrangements.	
		2.0 pm – 4.30 pm	Under Company arrangements.	
			2/LT. GLOVER reported and was posted to the battalion [D. Coy.] from 22ND. R.W.F. (Reserve Bn.)	
			D Coy. formed a raiding party. O.C. being Capt: G. THOMAS other officers 2/LT. K.G. EDWARDS and 2/LT. LACK. The party commenced special training in "raiding".	

R O Campbell Lt/Col
Comm 13th R W Fus

#353 Wt. W2544/1454 700,000 5/15 D. D. & L. A.D.S.S./Forms/C. 2118.

Army Form C. 2118.

Instructions regarding War Diaries and Intelligence Summaries are contained in F. S. Regs., Part II. and the Staff Manual respectively. Title pages will be prepared in manuscript.

WAR DIARY
or
INTELLIGENCE SUMMARY.
(Erase heading not required.)

Place	Date	Hour	Summary of Events and Information	Remarks and references to Appendices
'D' CAMP. A 30 a. 9. [illegible]	12/5/16.	6.45 AM – 7.30 AM	Physical Drill in conjunction with 15th R.W.F.	
		9.0 AM – [illegible]	Bayonet Fighting.	
		11.0 AM – 12.30 PM – 2.0–3.0 PM	Work under Company arrangements which included the issuing of the new SMALL BOX RESPIRATOR and drilling of the same. Company work and specialist training. Remainder of day the battalion rested owing to fatigue party being supplied at 4.30 PM for 11 hours fatigue on CANAL BANK DEFENCES. 3 Officers were detailed to report at [illegible] at [illegible] to receive instructions as to work on CANAL BANK.	
		11.0 PM	Party to [illegible] [illegible] fatigue was cancelled.	
	13/5/16.	6.45 AM	Physical Drill	
		9.0 AM	Bayonet Fighting	
		11.0 AM – 12.30 PM	Training under Company arrangements. Further practice in use of new RESPIRATOR [GAS]	
		2.0 – 3.0 PM	Training under Company arrangements. Fatigue as on 12/5/16, the party returning by buses at 2.0 AM following day [14/5/16.]	
	14/5/16.	AM – PM 6.45 – 12.30	Battalion rested owing to fatigues supplied previously [13/5/16.]	
		1.0 pm – 8.0 pm	Fatigues supplied for cutting brushwood.	
	15/5/16.	6.45 – 7.30 AM	Physical Drill in conjunction with LONDON WELSH. } Capt. Harg[illegible] granted LEAVE. [10 DAYS.]	
		9.0 AM	Bayonet Fighting.	
		10.0 AM – 12.30 PM	Training under Company arrangements.	
		1.0 PM – 7.0 PM	Three fatigue parties supplied for road-making and the construction of 'horse lines'.	
	16/5/16.	6.45 AM – 7.30 AM	Physical Drill. 9.0–9.45 AM. Bayonet Fighting [15th R.W.F.] Programme as on previous days. The C.O. returned from SPECIAL LEAVE.	

R D Campbell Lt Col
Com 13th R W Fus

#353 Wt. W2544/1454 700,000 5/15 D. D. & L. A.D.S.S./Forms/C. 2118.

Instructions regarding War Diaries and Intelligence Summaries are contained in F. S. Regs., Part II. and the Staff Manual respectively. Title pages will be prepared in manuscript.

WAR DIARY
or
INTELLIGENCE SUMMARY.
(*Erase heading not required.*)

Army Form C. 2118.

Place	Date	Hour	Summary of Events and Information	Remarks and references to Appendices
CHATEAU DES TROIS TOURS.	17/IX/16.	10·45 AM.	C of E parade service.	
		11·45 AM.	Welsh & English Nonconformists parade service.	
			2/LT. NAPTHALI reported on rejoining the battalion after 7 months SICK LEAVE and in hospital.	
			Battalion HQ and "C" Coy. moved to CHATEAU DES TROIS TOURS and took over from 14TH. R.W.F. A+B Coys. 13TH R.W.F. relieved 2 Coys. 14TH. R.W.F. at LANCASHIRE FARM and CANAL BANK EAST [A. Coy:] and CANAL BANK WEST, SOUTH of BRIDGE 4.	
	18/IX/16.		Fatigue parties supplied to R.E. dumps.	
	19/IX/16.		Raiding party brought up the line by buses. Raid to commence at 2·0 AM of the 20/IX/16. Gap made in enemy's wire by our Artillery in readiness for our raiders. LT. MORRIS proceeded on LEAVE. [10 days] to ENGLAND.	
	20/IX/16.	2·0 AM.	Intense bombardment on enemy's front line lasting until 2·4 AM. at which time raiding party prepared to enter Germans trenches. Heavy bombing by the enemy, whose front line trench seemed to be occupied by large numbers of Germans.	
	21/IX/16.		Fatigue parties supplied for night work as previously. 2/LTS. DANN, BOWDAGE, and GLOVER were attached to "raiders" for instruction in readiness for a second raid on the German front line.	
RIGHT SUB-SECTOR.	22/IX/16.	7·0 AM 5·0 PM.	Fatigue parties supplied.	
			The battalion relieved 14TH. R.W.F. in the RIGHT SUB-SECTOR, LEFT SECTOR. 1 Coy. 14TH. R.W.F. remained at SKIPTON POST as LEFT CENTRE COY. owing to "D" Coy. of this batt. being trained as a raiding party.	
	23/IX/16.	3·0 AM.	CAPT. G. THOMAS was wounded in the foot while on patrol in NOMANSLAND. LT. WYNNE EDWARDS was appointed as O.C. Raiders in the place of CAPT THOMAS. Quiet day with very little hostile firing of any description.	
		10·0 pm.	A patrol of 2 N.C.O's and 1 man left our lines at C.15.b 7.6½ and remained in NOMANSLAND for 2 hours (approx.) They had nothing to report, NOMANSLAND being void of both enemy patrols and working parties. — Considerable drainage was done during the day.	

R. W. Beningfield Lt Col
Comm 13th R.W. Fus.

8353 Wt. W2544/1454 700,000 5/15 D. D. & L. A.D.S.S./Forms/C. 2118.

G13/14

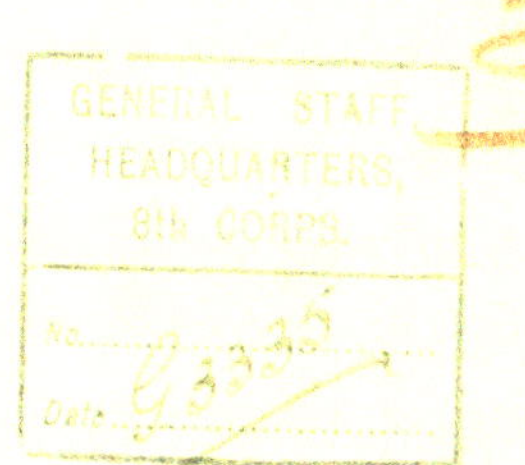

S E C R E T

REPORT ON RAID CARRIED OUT BY A PARTY OF THE 13TH BATTALION ROYAL WELSH FUSILIERS ON THE NIGHT 19/20th SEPTEMBER 1916

With a view to carrying out a raid on the German trenches at C.14.a.,4½.2 and obtaining identifications, a detachment of the 13th Battalion Royal Welsh Fusiliers was trained for this purpose previously. On the morning and afternoon of the 19th instant the wire was cut in two places near the selected point.

The party consisting of three officers, eight N.C.O's and 65 men under the Command of CAPTAIN GRASSER-THOMAS left our front trench at 1.20 a.m. and lined up in NO MAN'S LAND in front of our wire.

An Artillery barrage was formed at 2 a.m. on the point of entry and at 2.4 a.m. was raised on to the German Support line, and formed a pocket round the objective.

Just as the party started to advance it was bombed heavily from its left causing some casualties in the left party who were forced to move to the right, as the wire was not cut at the place where the Germans were bombing from. This threw the remainder of the party into confusion, and only some six managed to reach the gap in the wire which they were unable to go through owing to the German trench being strongly manned.

The party eventually had to withdraw without having affected its object. Casualties were 3 missing and 4 wounded.

Major General,

20/9/1916. Commanding 38th (Welsh) Division.

S E C R E T.

REPORT ON RAID CARRIED OUT BY 13TH R.W.F. ON NIGHT 28th/29th SEPTR. 1916.

C.14 a 4½. 2½

At 10-45.p.m. reconnoitring patrols that had been sent out returned, and reported the gap in the enemy's wire to be clear, but that the enemy was working in the trench behind.

The raiders got into NO MANS LAND without incident.

The Artillery bombardment opened at 11-30.p.m. and under cover of the dame the raiding party entered the German trench about C.14.a.4½.2½. The front trench at the point of entry was found to be unoccupied with the exception of 3 Germans who were killed. Papers were found upon one dead German, and were taken away by an officer, Lieut. LACK, who is missing. The Germans from a trench close behind the front trench, heavily bombed our raiding party. Two dugouts were found and searched and two valises and 2 waterbottles were obtained from them. These were lost with the officer who is missing.

No caps were worn by any of the Germans seen - they all wore steel helmets. There was no M.G. fire from the enemy, and the suspected machine gun was not found.

Our casualties amounted to 1 killed, 2 missing and 9 wounded as far as can be ascertained at present.

None of the missing have been recoovered though a search party was sent out to look for them.

C. G. Blackader Major General,

29-9-1916. Commanding 38th (Welsh) Division.

Instructions regarding War Diaries and Intelligence Summaries are contained in F. S. Regs., Part II. and the Staff Manual respectively. Title pages will be prepared in manuscript.

Army Form C. 2118.

WAR DIARY
or
INTELLIGENCE SUMMARY.

(Erase heading not required.)

Place	Date	Hour	Summary of Events and Information	Remarks and references to Appendices
RIGHT SUB-SECTOR	24/IX/16.	10.15 AM	A hostile plane attempted to cross our lines but was prevented by our anti aircraft guns.	A L/Cpl. of L.H.G. sect. was killed by enemy sniper.
		10.30 AM 11.30	Hostile shelling of our front line and DAWSON CITY. Shells used probably lighter than 77 mm.	
			Drainage at C 14 d 2.6. and thickening of parapet (new system) at C 14 c 7.6.	
	25/IX/16.		Building of new parapet at C 14 c 7½.6. and drainage at C 14 c 9.5. Gaps in parapet partly closed at C 14 a 3½.[illegible]	
		10.0 pm.	Medium T.M. fired [illegible] rounds at C 14 a 5½.1½. and the enemy retaliated with 4 rifle grenades.	
		5.0 pm 6.0	Hostile shelling of FUSILIER and [illegible] neighbourhood with 77 mm. – Reported that a considerable amount of enemy wire is hidden by the long grass. MAJOR LLOYD proceeded on LEAVE to ENGLAND.	
			A man was accidentally killed by one of our own men just after stand down [5.0 AM (B)]	
	26/IX/16.		Greater hostile activity than usual.	
		10.30 AM 5.0 P.M.	Our front line shelled with 77 mm. at C 14 d 1.5 and again with [illegible] in the afternoon.	
		9.0 P.M.	2/Lt. SEYMOUR [11th R.W.K.] left our line with a patrol at C 14 c 6.9. [illegible]	
	27/IX/16.		[illegible]	
			[illegible] GILBERT and [illegible] went out [illegible] patrol [illegible]. The party returned a little after midnight. Considerable drainage was carried out at C 14 c 6.½, C 14 c .6½. Thickening of	
		8 PM 5.30.	Parapet [new system] C 13 b 9½.2, C 14 c [illegible], and C 14 a 2.20. [illegible] was relieved by 11th R.W.K.	
		7.30.	D Coy. 11th R.W.K. relieving C Coy. of the Bn. at 5.30 pm. C Coy. 11th R.W.K. relieving A Coy. the Bn. at 7.30 pm. and B Coy. 11th Bn. R.W.K. relieving B Coy. the Bn. at 7.30 pm.	

R D Campbell
[illegible]

5353 Wt. W2544/1454 700,000 5/15 D. D. & L. A.D.S.S./Forms/C. 2118.

Instructions regarding War Diaries and Intelligence Summaries are contained in F. S. Regs., Part II. and the Staff Manual respectively. Title pages will be prepared in manuscript.

WAR DIARY
or
INTELLIGENCE SUMMARY.
(Erase heading not required.)

Army Form C. 2118.

Place	Date	Hour	Summary of Events and Information	Remarks and references to Appendices
CHATEAU DES TROIS TOURS.	28/IX/16		A raiding party consisting of 4 Officers, 10 N.C.O's & 63 men left here at 8.15 p.m. and reached the front line at 10.15 p.m. Artillery started intensive bombardment on enemy's line at 11.29 p.m. & kept this up for half an hour. The raiders succeeded in entering the enemy's trenches & were back in our lines by 12.10 a.m. 2nd Lieut JACK, who captured [illegible] papers, is unfortunately missing.	
	29/IX/16		Enemy retaliation was feeble.	
	30/IX/16		Fatigue parties [illegible] supplied to R.E.	

R D Campbell Lt Col
Comd 13th Batt Rl Ir Ris

8353 Wt. W2544/1454 700,000 5/15 D. D. & L. A.D.S.S./Forms/C. 2118.

Vol 11

WAR DIARY.

13TH. BATTALION.

ROYAL WELSH FUSILIERS.

OCTOBER 1916

Instructions regarding War Diaries and Intelligence Summaries are contained in F. S. Regs., Part II. and the Staff Manual respectively. Title pages will be prepared in manuscript.

WAR DIARY
or
INTELLIGENCE SUMMARY.
(Erase heading not required.)

Army Form C. 2118.

Place	Date	Hour	Summary of Events and Information	Remarks and references to Appendices
CHATEAU DES TROIS TOURS.	1/X/16.	P.M. 8.50.	The relief of 14TH. Bn. R.W.F. complete, the relief being commenced in day light.	
		11.0.	Enemy working party heard working on his wire at C.14.a.4.2. A Lewis Gun was fired in its direction and	
B.28.a.6.1½.		11.30.	seemingly terminated work in the area mentioned.	
CANAL BANK.			The evening was exceedingly quiet.	
C.19.C.4.4.	2/X/16.		Our parapet was built up and thickened at C.14.a½.2½.	
		A.M.	Considerable draining was done at C.14.c.6.6½.	
		9.0. 10.0.	Artillery activity to which the enemy retaliated by firing a number of T.M's. and by shelling to the left of HUDDERSFIELD COMCTN. TRENCH, but caused no damage.	
	3/X/16.	1AM–5.0AM.	The night was uneventful, occasional Hostile M.G. activity. During the day our Artillery cut the enemy's wire opposite the centre Company's front. There was not much hostile firing in retaliation.	
		3.30 pm	Enemy retaliated with 4.2's, prior to this he sent over 3, 77mm two of which were "duds".	
		3.45 pm	Very light or rocket [white] was sent up by the enemy opposite E25 shortly after, his T.M's started coming over – three T.M. guns being brought into play.	
	4/X/16.		During the night a very small number of Very lights was sent up by the enemy.	
			His MG's. were very quiet – on one occasion enemy threw 1 bomb in to his own wire opposite the left of the Centre Company.	
			Enemy again fired T.M's on front line right of EALING also on LANC. FM. – one man was very slightly wounded in the head by a fragment of T.M.	
	5/X/16.		Considerable work, chiefly drainage and repairing of front line, has been done during last two days. – EALING has been drained so that the level of the water is about 6 ins. lower than previously. Batt. relieved by 14TH. R.W.F. [see OP. ORDS.]	
	6/X/16.		Fatigue parties supplied by Coys. on Canal Banks EAST and WEST. – R.E. fatigues mostly.	

R D Campbell Lt Col
Comm 13th Batt R W Fus

#353 Wt. W2544/1454 700,000 5/15 D. D. & L. A.D.S.S./Forms/C. 2118.

Army Form C. 2118.

WAR DIARY
or
INTELLIGENCE SUMMARY.
(Erase heading not required.)

Instructions regarding War Diaries and Intelligence Summaries are contained in F. S. Regs., Part II. and the Staff Manual respectively. Title pages will be prepared in manuscript.

Place	Date	Hour	Summary of Events and Information	Remarks and references to Appendices
CHATEAU B.26.a.b.d.	7/x/16.		Fatigues supplied: enemy brought down one of our aeroplanes, & having done so centred his Artillery fire on it, but failed to do any more damage – subsequently the machine having been repaired – damage done being but a slight, the pilot was able to mount & fly away again.	
Canal Bank ? C.W.	8/x/16		Carrying fatigue for 113th. T.M.B. – a party of 72 men carried STOKES BOMBS to the front line – this in anticipation of the raid to be carried out by this Battalion.	
	9/x/16.	3.0 p.m.	Battalion relieved 14th. Bn. R.W.F. —	
		5.30 p.m.	C & D. Coys 13th. R.W.F. relieved LEFT Coy. 14th. R.W.F. at 3. p.m.	
			A & B. Coys 13th. R.W.F. relieved CENTRE Coy. 14th. R.W.F. at 5.30 p.m.	
			The RIGHT Coy. 14th. R.W.F. was not relieved.	
			Owing to it being daylight when relief was carried out, not more than 10 men were allowed to pass up HUDDERSFIELD at a time, each party of 10 men passed up at 5 minutes interval.	
			Lt VAUGHAN proceeded on leave to IRELAND and Lt. HARRIS took charge of A & B. Coys. 2/Lt. J. H. OWEN being i/c of C & D Coys. the remainder of the Batt. being in training for the raid.	
			The night was uneventful.	
	10/x/16.		Work, under R.E. supervision, was done in front line making new bays behind the old (original) bays. The line is in a fair condition, E-line being in a much better and cleaner condition.	
	11/x/16		Enemy fairly quiet during the day.	
	12/x/16.		The raid by this Batt. was carried out between 9.1 p.m. and 9.39 p.m.	
			The raid was under the direct supervision of CAPT. G. H. LEES.	
		P.M. 6.15	The Raiders consisted of 4 Officers, 11 N.C.O.'s, and 74 men. They left CHATEAU DES TROIS TOURS at 6.15 p.m. and were addressed by the Brigadier General Commanding at 7.13 p.m. on the CANAL BANK.	
		7.13 p.m.	And he wished them luck.	

2353 Wt. W2541/1454 700,000 5/15 D. D. & L. A.D.S.S./Forms/C. 2118.

Instructions regarding War Diaries and Intelligence Summaries are contained in F. S. Regs., Part II. and the Staff Manual respectively. Title pages will be prepared in manuscript.

WAR DIARY
or
INTELLIGENCE SUMMARY.
(*Erase heading not required.*)

Army Form C. 2118.

Place	Date	Hour	Summary of Events and Information	Remarks and references to Appendices
RIGHT SUB-SECTION LEFT SECTOR	11/3/16.	P.M. 8.45	The party formed up behind our parados between E.24. and E.25. at 8.45 p.m.	
		9.0.	At 9.p.m. which hour was ZERO the Artillery bombardment started, and at 9.1 p.m. the whole party	
		9.1.	rushed forward and reached the enemy's parapet just before 9.3 p.m. at which time the bombardment was scheduled to lift.	
			The raiders obtained 1 prisoner, a machine gun and some identifications. 15 of the enemy were accounted for.	
			We had no men killed, but 2/LTS. PATON and THOMAS were wounded rather seriously, and CAPT. LEES and C.S.M. F.J. BARRON were slightly wounded also a number of O.Rs.	
			The whole ~~was~~ is considered as a distinct success, and reflects great credit upon those who took part in it.	
	12/3/16.		The enemy retaliated rather heavily with T.Ms., presumably as a result of the raid upon his trenches, but during the day he was fairly quiet.	
	13/3/16.		Enemy sent a few T.Ms. over in the morning, in the afternoon he fired a few 4.2s. causing no damage whatsoever.	
	14/3/16.		2 Coys. of the 17TH. R.W.F. relieved the ~~three~~ Coys. of the 14TH. R.W.F at ~~[illegible]~~ LANC. FM. CANAL BANKS EAST and WEST. Enemy very quiet during the day.	
	15/3/16.	P.M. 5.45	The Batt: was relieved by the 17TH. BN. R.W.Fus.	
			A&B Coys. 13TH. R.W.F. were relieved by D. Coy. 17TH. R.W.F. at 5.45 p.m.	
			X Coy. 13TH. R.W.F. was relieved by C. Coy. 17TH. R.W.F. at 6.0. p.m.	
			C&D Coys. 13TH. R.W.F. were relieved by A. Coy. 17TH. R.W.F. at 5.30 p.m.	
			The routes followed were.—	
			D. Coy. 17TH. R.W.F.-LANCASHIRE RAILWAY.	
			C. " " " " " HUDDERSFIELD TRENCH.	
				R. C. Campbell [illegible] Com. 13th Batt. R.W.Fus.

#353 Wt. W2544/1454 700,000 5/15 D. D. & L. A.D.S.S./Forms/C. 2118.

Instructions regarding War Diaries and Intelligence Summaries are contained in F. S. Regs., Part II. and the Staff Manual respectively. Title pages will be prepared in manuscript.

WAR DIARY
or
INTELLIGENCE SUMMARY.
(Erase heading not required.)

Army Form C. 2118.

Place	Date	Hour	Summary of Events and Information	Remarks and references to Appendices
"D" CAMP A.30.	16/5/16.	1.0AM.	After being relieved the Coys. of this Batt. proceeded independently to "D" Camp. On arrival the men rejoined their respective Companies, and occupied the same Huts as on previous occasion. X Coy. was composed of the raiders. The Battalion rested for the day. Rifle inspection by Coys. in the afternoon.	NB. 17/5/16. The Batt. was inspected by the ARMY COMMANDER. During "clean fatigue" the GENERAL presented the M.M. to NCOs & men of the 15th [illegible] R.W.F. "Raiders".
	17/5/16.	7.0AM 2.0PM	Physical Drill. – 9.30AM. B. Fighting 10.15AM – 12.30 pm. under Coy. arrangements. Specialists training under Coy. arrangements.	
	18/5/16.		Programme as on previous day. Fatigue, for buried cable on CANAL BANK, supplied.	
	19/5/16.		No early morning parade owing to fatigue – men resting. 9.30 AM. onwards parades as previously.	
	20/5/16.	7.0AM.	Physical Drill and parades as before. Specialists training. Fatigue parties supplied [R.E.]	
	21/5/16.		No early morning parade owing to fatigues until 9 AM. Other parades as previously.	
	22/5/16.	11.0AM	Noncomf. Welsh & English parade, and at 2.30pm. Church Parade, most of the Batt. being on fatigue.	
	23/5/16.		Battalion inspected by Corps Commander [VIII Corps] who presented CAPT. G.H. LEES with M.C. [CAPT. LEES was in command of the Raiders 14/5/16]	
CHATEAU DES TROIS TOURS	24/5/16.	P.M. 4.45. 6.40.	Batt. relieved 17TH. R.W.F at the CHATEAU and CANAL BANKS EAST and WEST. Batt. was under orders of the G.O.C. 115TH. BRIGADE.	Capt. G.H. Lees & 2/Lt. V. [illegible] ([illegible]) presented [illegible] 24/5/16.
	25/5/16.	10.0P.M.	G.O.C. 113TH. INF. BDE. assumed command of the LEFT BDE. SECTOR on completion of relief 25/26/5. 13TH. Bn. R.W.F. relieved 16TH. Bn. WELCH REGT in the RIGHT SUB SECTOR. Relief complete at 2.0AM.	

2353 Wt. W2544/1454 700,000 5/15 D.D. & L. A.D.S.S./Forms/C. 2118.

S E C R E T 13 RWF October 1916 38th Division No. G.S.483 9

VIII Corps

REPORT ON RAID CARRIED OUT BY 13TH ROYAL WELSH FUSILIERS ON NIGHT 12th/13th OCTOBER 1916. C.14.a.4½.2

Last night a raiding party of four Officers and 67 Other Ranks of the 13th Battalion Royal Welsh Fusiliers entered the German trenches at C.14.a.,4½.2 with the object of killing or capturing Germans and obtaining identifications.

Previous to the raid taking place a gap had been cut in the hostile wire by Trench Mortar and Artillery fire.

At 9 p.m. an Artillery bombardment opened on the German line at the spot to be raided, and the raiders moved forward under cover of our fire. At 9.3 p.m. our bombardment lifted on to the German support line, and a barrage was formed on either flank - at the same time the raiders rushed the German trench.

There was a little hostile Artillery and Machine Gun fire, but the hostile Trench Mortar fire was heavy, and caused some casualties amongst the raiding party.

Only one German dugout was entered, and this was empty.

A hostile Machine Gun was found which continued to fire until all the team were killed.

The hostile trenches were much damaged by our Artillery and Trench Mortar bombardment, and some wounded Germans were found in the trenches.

The signal to withdraw was given at 9.16 p.m., and all the raiding party were back in our trenches at 9.20 p.m. having brought back the hostile Machine Gun and one slightly wounded prisoner of the 2nd Guards Reserve Regiment.

Our casualties (as far as is known at present) are :-

1 Other Rank killed
7 Officers and 17 Other Ranks slightly wounded.

The enemy's casualties are estimated at, at least,

12 killed
1 prisoner
and an unknown number of wounded.

REPORT ON RAID CARRIED OUT BY THE 15TH BATTALION WELSH REGIMENT ON NIGHT 14th/15th OCTOBER 1916 ON THE MORTALDJE SAP

Last night a raiding party of the 15th Battalion Welsh Regiment entered the MORTALDJE SAP. The Sap was found deserted and more or less derelict.

No identifications were obtained.

The Officer Commanding the raiding party on finding this to be the case attempted to enter the German front line trench, but the hostile wire, ~~however~~ was found too strong, and as the mats for crossing hostile wire had all been used in entering the MORTALDJE SAP there were none left to cross the wire in front of the German front line trench, Consequently the party had to withdraw, and returned to our lines without casualties.

Major General,
15/10/1916. Commanding 38th (Welsh) Division.

Instructions regarding War Diaries and Intelligence Summaries are contained in F. S. Regs., Part II. and the Staff Manual respectively. Title pages will be prepared in manuscript.

WAR DIARY
or
INTELLIGENCE SUMMARY.
(Erase heading not required.)

Army Form C. 2118.

Place	Date	Hour	Summary of Events and Information	Remarks and references to Appendices
CANAL BANK C19.C.4.4.	26/2/16.	4.0AM	Relief complete. Prior to relieving, the Batt. was on carrying fatigue from Bridge 6 to extreme left of the LEFT SECTOR carrying STOKES MORTAR ammunition. Hence the reason for relief so late.	
	27/2/16.		Enemy exceptionally quiet, due, no doubt, to the fact that the enemy has had a relief in his line. Patrols under charge of 2/LTS MILES, THOMAS, and BOWDAGE reported all quiet in NOMAN'S LAND. These patrols were – fighting patrols from 12 to 16 in number.	
	28/2/16.	11.0AM	Enemy Trench Mortars active about LANC FM. Hostile shelling about HEADINGLY to the right of Right Coy. HQ. [77 mm.] no damage done. He also shelled PIONEER working party working on HUDDERSFIELD TRENCH [77 MM.] wounding one man slightly. New bays were completed in front line and occupied by our men, the old bays in front of the new ones were filled in. A great deal of drainage has been done, the level of water and slush in some places having been lowered by 1 foot.	
	29/2/16.		The enemy was again active with his T.Ms, and took a great deal of Artillery retaliation to silence him. EALING is still in a very bad condition, it being almost impossible to get up to the front line by day, it is certainly not safe to allow men to go up this trench individually. The depth and the nature of the water and slush being so great and bad. The 16TH. R.W.F. carried out a successful raid on the German trenches capturing 4 of the enemy, suffering very few and slight casualties themselves. The enemy retaliated on the left and centre companies, though the raid was carried out on the left of the LEFT SUB-SECTION. All TELEPONE WIRES to CENTRE and RIGHT Companies were broken by hostile shells & T.M.s. – The entrance to HEADINGLY and EALING trenches was completely blocked owing to the enemy T.M. dropping there.	

353 Wt. W2544/1454 700,000 5/15 D. D. & L. A.D.S.S./Forms/C. 2118.

Instructions regarding War Diaries and Intelligence Summaries are contained in F. S. Regs., Part II. and the Staff Manual respectively. Title pages will be prepared in manuscript.

WAR DIARY
or
INTELLIGENCE SUMMARY.
(Erase heading not required.)

Army Form C. 2118.

Place	Date	Hour	Summary of Events and Information	Remarks and references to Appendices
CANAL BANK RIGHT SUB-SECTION.	30/x/16.	1.0 AM	Patrols were sent out [officer fighting patrol] into NOMANS LAND and reported all normal and quiet. – The day was very quiet, continuous work was done on EALING, NILE and SKIPTON also on HARDWELY – draining and clearing these trenches and relaying trench boards where possible.	During 29/30 enemy's retaliation 1 man was killed and 2 men wounded. All three were Lewis Gunners and of the same team.
C.19.c.4.4.		P.M. 9.45	The BATT. was relieved by 14th. Bn. R.W.F: relief complete being report at 9.45 pm. 2/Lt. T. M. OWEN proceeded on LEAVE to ENGLAND.	
CHATEAU DES TROIS TOURS.	31/x/16.		Fatigue parties supplied to the line and R.E. dumps for carrying. Day uneventful.	

2353 Wt. W2544/1454 700,000 5/15 D. D. & L. A.D.S.S./Forms/C. 2118.

WAR DIARY

Vol 12

13th BATTALION

ROYAL WELSH FUSILIERS

NOVEMBER 1916

Instructions regarding War Diaries and Intelligence Summaries are contained in F. S. Regs., Part II. and the Staff Manual respectively. Title pages will be prepared in manuscript.

WAR DIARY
or
INTELLIGENCE SUMMARY.
(Erase heading not required.)

Army Form C. 2118.

Place	Date	Hour	Summary of Events and Information	Remarks and references to Appendices
	[illegible]		[illegible] the Q.rs and C Coy at CHATEAU des TROIS TOURS [illegible] companies at CANAL BANKS – EAST and WEST and 2 [illegible] of A Coy [illegible] LANCASHIRE FARM.	
	2.XI.16		[illegible] the day was very quiet.	
	3.XI.16		[illegible] side. One of our OBSERVATION BALLOONS was seen [illegible] the top of the CHATEAU in a N.E direction – the anti aircraft guns of both sides fired a great deal at the balloon but failed to bring it down. Two or three aeroplanes were seen near it, but they evidently failed to bring it down.	
	4.XI.16.		A great deal of activity on the part of our artillery during the afternoon. Battalion was relieved by [illegible] Bn R W [illegible] in the RIGHT SUB-SECTION the relief being complete at 6.50 p.m. 2nd LIEUT [illegible] proceeded to England on leave.	

W 2353 Wt W25.../1454 700,000 5/15 D. D. & L. A.D.S.S./Forms/C 2118.

Instructions regarding War Diaries and Intelligence Summaries are contained in F. S. Regs., Part II. and the Staff Manual respectively. Title pages will be prepared in manuscript.

WAR DIARY
or
INTELLIGENCE SUMMARY.
(*Erase heading not required.*)

Army Form C. 2118.

Place	Date	Hour	Summary of Events and Information	Remarks and references to Appendices
	15 XI 16		Found small Working Party for 4 hours work on CANAL BANK Defences. Relieved 10th Batt S.W.B. in the front line Right Sub-sector Right Sector.	
	16-17 XI 16		Exceedingly quiet during the 48 hours.	
	17/18 XI 16		Heavy bombardment of enemy line near HIGH COMMAND REDOUBT in which guns of all calibres participated. Severe bombardments took place also at 6pm and 11pm, and at the latter hour a successful raid was carried out by the 14th Batt Welsh Regiment who were on our left. The result of the raid was a considerable number of prisoners and a machine gun. Much damage was done to the hostile trenches and strong points.	
	18 XI 16		No hostile retaliation for bombardments of previous day. Nothing of any note happened.	
	19 XI 16		Subjected to some fire from an enfilade gun thought to be firing from the neighbourhood of HOOGE. No damage was done.	
	20 XI 16		Were relieved by the 13th Battalion Welsh Regiment in our position. Relief complete by 7.50 pm. Battalion entrained at YPRES for BRANDHOEK, whence we marched to E Camp which was taken over from 15th Batt RWF. On arrival in Camp came under orders of G.O.C. 113th Infy Brigade.	
	21 XI 16		Rested. Kit inspection and general clean up after 26 days in the forward area.	
	22 XI 16		Training. Found Working Parties for Buried Cable Work in the forward area.	
	23 XI 16		Training. Brigade Competitions. Considerable keenness was shown and competitions were successful. Found 350 men for Buried Cable Work. 100 by day and 250 by night. Test Alarm at 10am.	
	24 XI 16		Relieved 17th Batt RWF in the Right Reserve position Right Sector. Relief reported complete at 9.50pm.	
	25 XI 16		Batt HQ at Chateau des TROIS TOURS also 6 platoons remainder of Battalion as follows – 1 Coy Canal Bank West, 2 Platoons Canal Bank East and 1 Coy. at LANCASHIRE FARM.	
	26 XI 16		Found Working parties for Front line work and work on Dugouts and a carrying party.	
	27 XI 16		Same parties as for previous day. Retaliatory bombardment commencing at about 7.35 which lasted for about 45 mts. S.O.S was sent up by Left Battalion. Batteries barraged the enemy lines in their respective Zones.	R. Campbell Lt Col Comdg 13th Batt RWF

2353 Wt. W2544/1454 700,000 5/15 D. D. & L. A.D.S.S./Forms/C. 2118.

Army Form C. 2118.

Instructions regarding War Diaries and Intelligence Summaries are contained in F. S. Regs., Part II and the Staff Manual respectively. Title pages will be prepared in manuscript.

WAR DIARY
or
INTELLIGENCE SUMMARY.
(Erase heading not required.)

Place	Date	Hour	Summary of Events and Information	Remarks and references to Appendices

£353 Wt W2541/1454 700,000 5/15 D. D. & L. A.D.S.S./Forms/C 2118.

13th BATTN ROYAL WELSH FUSILIERS

Vol 13

WAR DIARY

FOR

. DECEMBER 1916 .

Army Form C. 2118.

WAR DIARY
or
INTELLIGENCE SUMMARY.
(Erase heading not required.)

Instructions regarding War Diaries and Intelligence Summaries are contained in F. S. Regs., Part II. and the Staff Manual respectively. Title pages will be prepared in manuscript.

Place	Date	Hour	Summary of Events and Information	Remarks and references to Appendices

#353 Wt. W2544/1454 700,000 5/15 D. D. & L. A.D.S.S./Forms/C. 2118.

Instructions regarding War Diaries and Intelligence Summaries are contained in F. S. Regs., Part II. and the Staff Manual respectively. Title pages will be prepared in manuscript.

WAR DIARY
or
INTELLIGENCE SUMMARY.
(Erase heading not required.)

Army Form C. 2118.

Place	Date	Hour	Summary of Events and Information	Remarks and references to Appendices
	10th.		Relieved 14th Batt. R.W.F. relief being over by 5.55 pm. LANCASHIRE FARM was heavily shelled during relief, from 5 pm – 5.30 pm. The relieved unit suffered some casualties, but we escaped. The enemy also put a few heavy shells into his own line: this immediately produced a rocket which burst into a green & pink stars. Artillery fire was then lengthened. This occurred 3 times. Considerable amount of wire put out. Nothing of note occurred during the night.	[initials]
	11th.		Enemy's artillery quiet, though our guns did considerable registration. As a test 2 red rockets were sent up from each Coy front at 9 pm all went off successfully. Hostile Working Party was dispersed on our front by Lewis Gun fire. An unusual number of Very lights sent up by enemy, most of them from his third line or thereabouts. 20 yds of good wire was put out on our right front. As an innovation parades were carried out in the front line — Physical and bayonet exercises, gas helmet drill and musketry were performed.	[initials] [initials]
	12th.		Exceedingly wet and quiet day. All labour was disposed of in clearing falls.	
	13th.		Quiet day. Divisional relief commenced in front line. Battalion was relieved in Right Front position Centre Brigade by 16th Batt Sherwood Foresters. The relief which was well conducted was over by 6.35 pm. Later the 17th Batt K.R.R. relieved Battalion in the Right Reserve position on the Canal Bank. Companies proceeded independently to YPRES where we entrained for POPERINGHE. Arrived there at about 11.15 pm. Comfortable billets were found for the night.	[initials]
	14th.		Battalion assembled at Cheese Market station POPERINGHE and entrained in two trains for BOLLEZEELE where we arrived at 1.10 pm. Billets arranged for beforehand were found to be good though somewhat crowded so far as the men were concerned. Remainder of day spent in adjusting billets.	[initials]
	15th.		Day spent in cleaning up after 4 months in forward area. everyone very cheerful at prospect of spending Xmas in comfort. Brigadier General Commanding visited billets and expressed himself as being pleased with appearance of men & cleanliness of billets.	[initials]

B353 Wt. W2544/1454 700,000 5/15 D. D. & L. A.D.S.S./Forms/C. 2118.

Instructions regarding War Diaries and Intelligence Summaries are contained in F. S. Regs., Part II and the Staff Manual respectively. Title pages will be prepared in manuscript.

WAR DIARY

or

INTELLIGENCE SUMMARY.

(Erase heading not required.)

Army Form C. 2118.

Place	Date	Hour	Summary of Events and Information	Remarks and references to Appendices

2353 Wt W2544/1454 700,000 5/15 D. D. & L. A.D.S.S./Forms/C 2118.

Army Form C. 2118.

Instructions regarding War Diaries and Intelligence Summaries are contained in F. S. Regs., Part II. and the Staff Manual respectively. Title pages will be prepared in manuscript.

WAR DIARY
or
INTELLIGENCE SUMMARY.

(Erase heading not required.)

Place	Date	Hour	Summary of Events and Information	Remarks and references to Appendices
	27th.		Two Battalion attack scheme set by Brigade. H.Qrs. carried out in conjunction with 15th Batt. R.W.F. Situations were set by Brigade Major and G.S.O.2. Trench Mortars cooperated, as did also the Machine Gun Coy. During afternoon training was carried out under Battalion arrangements.	H.L.L.
	28th.		Same attack as above carried out by 14th & 16th Batts. R.W.F. The Battalion supplied the skeleton enemy. Battalion Drill & Musketry carried out under Battalion arrangements. 2 Officers and 50 O.R. sent out to fill in trenches which had been dug.	H.L.L.
	29th.		Cleaning up billets prior to move to "D" Camp (Forward area)	H.L.L.
	30th.		Relieved in rest area by 17th Batt. R.W. Fus. and then proceeded by train from BOLLEZEELE to POPERINGHE, whence Batt. marched to "D" Camp arriving at 3.30 pm	
	31st.		Sunday. No training. Church Parade. Working party of 1 Officer & 25 O.R. found for Camouflage Work.	

[illegible] Major.
Commanding 13th Bn. R.W.Fus.

2353 Wt. W2544/1454 700,000 5/15 D. D. & L. A.D.S.S./Forms/C. 2118.

WAR DIARY Vol 14

FOR

JANUARY 1917

13TH BATTN. ROYAL WELSH FUSILIERS

14.B
5 Mar

Instructions regarding War Diaries and Intelligence Summaries are contained in F. S. Regs., Part II. and the Staff Manual respectively. Title pages will be prepared in manuscript.

WAR DIARY
or
INTELLIGENCE SUMMARY.
(Erase heading not required.)

Army Form C. 2118.

Place	Date	Hour	Summary of Events and Information	Remarks and references to Appendices
In the Field	1st.		Training in D Camp. Nothing of note occurred, though the enemy considerably shelled some points well behind the line. Our artillery replied vigorously.	
	2nd.		Training in D Camp. Sent 1 Officer + 50 O.R. to YPRES to act as carrying party and [illegible] work in conjunction with the Field Coy attached to centre Brigade	
	3rd.		Sent 1 Officer and 25 O.R. to assist the party sent to YPRES yesterday. Also a party of 2 Officers and 100 O.R. to Canal Bank for work on dugouts.	
	4th.		Training at D Camp. Played off 1st round of football competition. C Coy v D Coy result D 7 C O.	
	5th.		Training at D Camp. Sent 1 Officer + 50 to carry R.E. material from AUSTERLITZ to MARENGO.	
	6th.		Training at D Camp. Carried out some recreational training in Bayonet fighting. Weather very bad.	
	7th.		No training. Church Parades.	
	8th.		Training at D Camp. Relieved [illegible] Company on the Canal Bank. Capt AUBERTIN returned after 3 months course in England.	
	9th.		Training at D Camp	
	10th.		Training at D Camp. A Coy carried out recreational training in musketry and Bayonet Fighting	[illegible] Major Comdg. 13th Bn R.W.F.

#353 Wt. W2544/1454 700,000 5/15 D. D. & L. A.D.S.S./Forms/C. 2118.

Army Form C. 2118.

Instructions regarding War Diaries and Intelligence Summaries are contained in F. S. Regs., Part II. and the Staff Manual respectively. Title pages will be prepared in manuscript.

WAR DIARY
or
INTELLIGENCE SUMMARY.
(Erase heading not required.)

Place	Date	Hour	Summary of Events and Information	Remarks and references to Appendices

#353 Wt. W2544/1454 700,000 5/15 D. D. & L. A.D.S.S./Forms/C. 2118.

Instructions regarding War Diaries and Intelligence Summaries are contained in F. S. Regs., Part II. and the Staff Manual respectively. Title pages will be prepared in manuscript.

WAR DIARY
or
INTELLIGENCE SUMMARY.

(Erase heading not required.)

Army Form C. 2118.

Place	Date	Hour	Summary of Events and Information	Remarks and references to Appendices
	22.		[illegible] all available men [illegible] Canal Bank [illegible] 14th Batt R.W.F. [illegible] support line [illegible] 22 [illegible]	[signature] Major. Comdg. 13th Bn. R.W.F.
	23.		[illegible] Nothing of importance happened this day.	
	24.		[illegible] Brigade. [illegible] 2 Companies; support line two Companies. The dispositions were found to work very well. [illegible]	
	25.		[illegible] shelling [illegible]	
	26.		[illegible] Railway. Considerable artillery activity by both sides. [illegible] Information was received that [illegible] additional precautions [illegible] taken [illegible] NO MANS LAND [illegible]	
	27.		[illegible] artillery activity. Officers and N.C.Os [illegible] X line.	
	28.		Enemy heavily shelled trenches in the neighbourhood of [illegible]. Relieved by 14th Batt. [illegible]: relief complete by 7.0 p.m.	
	29.		[illegible] Companies on the Canal Bank [illegible] at POPERINGHE.	

8353 Wt. W2544/1454 700,000 5/15 D. D. & L. A.D.S.S./Forms/C. 2118.

Army Form C. 2118.

Instructions regarding War Diaries and Intelligence Summaries are contained in F. S. Regs., Part II. and the Staff Manual respectively. Title pages will be prepared in manuscript.

WAR DIARY
or
INTELLIGENCE SUMMARY.

(Erase heading not required.)

Place	Date	Hour	Summary of Events and Information	Remarks and references to Appendices

2353 Wt. W1522/1454 700,000 5/15 D. D. & L. A.D.S.S./Forms/C 2118

Vol 15

WAR DIARY

15th BATTn RWF

FEBRUARY 1917.

15 B.

Instructions regarding War Diaries and Intelligence Summaries are contained in F. S. Regs., Part II. and the Staff Manual respectively. Title pages will be prepared in manuscript.

Army Form C. 2118.

WAR DIARY
or
INTELLIGENCE SUMMARY.
(Erase heading not required.)

Place	Date	Hour	Summary of Events and Information	Remarks and references to Appendices
In the field	1-2-17.		Heavy bombardment of enemy's lines in the BOESINGHE SECTOR by Corps Heavy Artillery and Divisional artillery from 8AM to 5PM. Enemy retaliated a little – mostly on our batteries. – The 13th Batt R.W.Fus relieved the 14th Bn R.W.Fus in the Right Sub-section of the Centre Brigade. – Companies of the 13 Bn R.W.Fus took up the following disposition on relief "A" Coy – RIGHT FRONT "D" Coy – LEFT FRONT "B" Coy – RIGHT SUPPORT. "C" Coy – LEFT SUPPORT. – Relief complete 6-30 P.M.	
" " "	2-2-17.		Enemy artillery shelled our back areas during the early hours of the morning. – Our artillery retaliated freely and shelled enemy's front and support lines intermittently throughout the day.	
" " "	3-2-17.		At 5-5AM our artillery opened an intense bombardment on and around CAESAR'S NOSE lasting till 5-6 A.M. No retaliation on the part of the enemy. – About 4PM enemy sent over several heavy shells on to the CANAL BANK but no damage done. Our artillery retaliated freely. Aerial activity was very marked throughout the day. Visibility good.	
" " "	4-2-17.		Very quiet day. – Wind changed S.E. during the afternoon and weather became misty. Night quiet.	
" " "	5-2-17.		Aerial activity very marked on both sides. – Visibility poor during the morning when artillery was quiet. The afternoon became clear and our artillery was active. Our French Mortars registered on CAESAR'S NOSE at 3PM. – The 13th Bn R.W.Fus was relieved by the 14th Batt R.W.Fus in the Right Subsection of the Centre Brigade – Relief complete 6-45 P.M. – The following dispositions were taken up on relief by the 13 R.W.Fus. – "A" Coy at TROIS TOURS. "B" Coy entrained for POPERINGE at 6-30 P.M. C & D Coys. CANAL BANK EAST.	
" " "	6-2-17.		The 38th Divisional Artillery in conjunction with the VIII Corps Heavy Artillery bombarded the hostile defences in the KRUPP SALIENT and trenches around LANCASHIRE FARM – no serious damage done from 9AM to 4PM. Enemy retaliated slightly on our front line. Our artillery again bombarded the KRUPP SALIENT from 9-30 P.M. to 9-45 P.M. – No retaliation on part of enemy.	
" " "	7-2-17.		Our artillery very active throughout the day. – Enemy's artillery quiet. – Considerable aerial activity throughout the day. – "B" Coy 13th R W Fus returned from POPERINGE.	
" " "	8-2-16		Enemy retaliated for our previous bombardments with heavy shelling on our front lines – No serious damage done. Our artillery retaliated freely.	
" " "	9-2-16		Enemy artillery active during the afternoon mostly on our back areas. – Several heavy shells were fired into BRIELEN. Our artillery fairly active throughout the day. – The 13th Bn. R.W.Fus relieved the 14th Bn R.W.Fus in the Right Subsection of the centre Brigade. – On relief the following dispositions were taken up by Coys. 13th Bn R.W.Fus. – "B" Coy – RIGHT FRONT "C" Coy – LEFT FRONT. "A" Coy – RIGHT SUPPORT "D" Coy – LEFT SUPPORT	
" " "	10-2-16		Quiet day. Very little hostile artillery activity on our front. – About 10 P.M. enemy artillery opened an intense bombardment on our lines in the neighbourhood of WILLTJE lasting for several minutes. – Our artillery retaliated freely.	

2353 Wt. W2544/1454 700,000 5/15 D. D. & L. A.D.S.S./Forms/C. 2118.

Army Form C. 2118.

Instructions regarding War Diaries and Intelligence Summaries are contained in F. S. Regs., Part II. and the Staff Manual respectively. Title pages will be prepared in manuscript.

WAR DIARY
or
INTELLIGENCE SUMMARY.
(Erase heading not required.)

Place	Date	Hour	Summary of Events and Information	Remarks and references to Appendices
In the field	11-2-17.		Very little artillery activity on our front during the day. - About 10 P.M. enemy sent a large number of light shells on to the CANAL BANK and around ESSEX FARM. - no damage done. - Hostile machine guns very quiet during the night.	
" " "	12-2-17.		Enemy again shelled CANAL BANK about 5 A.M. - After 10 A.M. enemy sent several Trench Mortars on to our front line, slight damage done to EALING and SKIPTON TRENCH. - Our artillery retaliated freely. - Throughout the day artillery on both sides were active. - Enemy bombarded CANAL BANK in the neighbourhood of BRIDGE VI about 6 P.M. for 15 minutes. Our Divisional in conjunction with the Corps Heavy Artillery retaliated freely.	
" " "	13-2-17.		Enemy Trench Mortars very active on our front line between 9 A.M. & 11 A.M. - damage done to EALING and also parapet in front line. Our artillery retaliated vigorously. - The 13th Bn. R.W.Fus. relieved by the 14th R.W.Fus. in the Right Subsection Centre Brigade - relief complete 8-15 P.M. Coys of the 13th R.W.Fus. took up the following dispositions on relief. A & B Coys. CANAL BANK E. - 'B' Coy. proceeded to POPERINGHE - 'D' Coy - TROIS TOURS.	
" " "	14-2-17.		Corps Heavy Artillery and Centre Group Artillery carried out a bombardment on certain points in the enemy's line from 10 A.M. - 4 P.M. - Enemy retaliated mostly on our batteries.	
" " "	15-2-17.		Centre Group and Corps Heavy artillery continued the bombardment on enemy's front from 10 A.M. - 4 P.M. - No retaliation on part of the enemy. 'C' Coy. returned from POPERINGHE.	
" " "	16-2-17.		Corps Heavy Artillery and Centre Group Artillery carried out a bombardment on certain points in enemy's lines between the hours of 10 AM and 4 PM. Visibility being poor, hostile artillery was quiet. A few shells were fired into BRIELEN.	
" " "	17-2-17.		Our artillery was very active during the afternoon, although visibility poor. - The 13th Bn. R.W.Fus. relieved the 14th R.W.Fus. in the Right Sub-section, Centre Brigade. - On relief, Coys. 13th R.W.Fus took up the following dispositions 'B' Coy. - RIGHT FRONT. - 'C' Coy LEFT FRONT 'A' Coy - RIGHT SUPPORT, 'D' Coy - LEFT SUPPORT. - Relief complete 8-10 P.M. - New Batt. Headquarters taken over - CANAL BANK WEST (C.25.a.9½.3¼).	
" " "	18-2-17.	......	At 3-19 A.M. a raiding party of the 14th R.W.Fus. entered enemy's trenches at C.14.a.3½.4. under cover of an intense bombardment. - Enemy retaliated vigorously on our front and support lines. Visibility being poor very little further activity on our front.	
" " "	19-2-17.		Our artillery active throughout the day, although visibility very poor. - In retaliation enemy sent over frequently light shells on our front and support lines.	
" " "	20-2-17.		Quiet throughout the day. - Heavy bombardment from 4 - 6-30 P.M. could be heard south of the salient. - 8 new officers arrived.	
" " "	21-2-17.		Very quiet owing to a thick mist rendering visibility observation impossible. - The 13th R.W.Fus. relieved by the 14th Bn. R.W.Fus in the Right Subsection of the Centre Brigade. - Relief complete at 6-30 P.M. - On relief Coys. of 13th R.W.Fus. took up the following dispositions - 'A' Coy. entrained for POPERINGHE - 'B' & 'C' Coys. - CANAL BANK EAST. 'D' Coy. CHATEAU des TROIS TOURS.	
" " "	22-2-17.		Artillery very quiet owing to poor visibility. - thick mist throughout the day.	
" " "	23-2-17.		No activity on the front. - visibility very poor. thick mist which cleared slightly during the afternoon.	

[signature] Major
Commanding 13th Bn. R.W. Fusiliers

2353 Wt. W2544/1454 700,000 5/15 D. D. & L. A.D.S.S./Forms/C. 2118.

Army Form C. 2118.

WAR DIARY
or
INTELLIGENCE SUMMARY.
(Erase heading not required.)

Instructions regarding War Diaries and Intelligence Summaries are contained in F. S. Regs., Part II. and the Staff Manual respectively. Title pages will be prepared in manuscript.

Place	Date	Hour	Summary of Events and Information	Remarks and references to Appendices
[illegible]	[illegible]		[illegible]	
[illegible]	[illegible]		[illegible]	

2353 Wt W2544/1454 700,000 5/15 D. D. & L. A.D.S.S./Forms/C 2118

13th BATTn ROYAL WELSH FUSILIERS

Vol 16

— WAR DIARY —

FOR

MARCH 1917

16 B
4 sheets

Instructions regarding War Diaries and Intelligence Summaries are contained in F. S. Regs., Part II. and the Staff Manual respectively. Title pages will be prepared in manuscript.

WAR DIARY
or
INTELLIGENCE SUMMARY.
(Erase heading not required.)

Army Form C. 2118.

Place	Date	Hour	Summary of Events and Information	Remarks and references to Appendices
In the field	[illegible]	—	Visibility very good. Artillery on both sides moderately active. Considerable aerial activity during the afternoon. 6 of our battle 'planes patrolled over enemy's lines from 2 to 3 PM and no hostile fire was brought to bear upon them. The 13th Bn R.W.Fus. was relieved by the 10th Bn Welsh Regiment in the Right Subsection of the Right Brigade – relief complete 6-10 PM. On relief Coys of the 13th R.W.Fus. took up the following dispositions – A B C & D Coys – CANAL BANK EAST. – One man [illegible] wounded.	Llewellyn Major. Commanding 13th Bn. R.W.Fusrs.
"	" 5th "	—	Visibility [illegible] – Situation quiet during the morning. From 2 – 3.45 PM our artillery and trench mortar batteries fired on the enemy [illegible] – slight retaliation by the enemy. Heavy artillery fire could be heard on the right from 11 PM to 12 midnight.	
	" 6th "	—	Visibility poor. Situation quiet during the morning – slight hostile activity during the afternoon.	
	" 7th "	—	Visibility poor during the morning – slightly clearer during the afternoon. From [illegible] PM enemy shelled our batteries [illegible]	
"	" 8th "	—	Very quiet day – visibility good – The 13th Bn R.W.Fus. [illegible] the 10th Bn Welsh Regiment in the Right Subsection of the Right Brigade – relief complete 7 PM.	
"	" 9th "	—	Enemy artillery and trench mortar batteries very active between 3 & 4 PM on our front and support lines – causing slight damage. [illegible] our artillery retaliated freely. [illegible] aerial activity between [illegible] 2-4 PM – 9 of our aeroplanes patrolled [illegible] for a considerable time [illegible] aerial [illegible] and three [illegible] in the [illegible] to be enemy's – Night very quiet.	
"	" 10th "	—	Visibility good. Very little activity on the front [illegible]	
	" 11th "	—	[illegible] during the early part of the morning and also at intervals during the day. The period [illegible] during which visibility was very good – very little [illegible] the front.	
	" 12th "	—	Very little artillery activity on the front – The 13th Bn R.W.Fus. relieved by the 10th Bn Welsh Regiment in the Right subsection of the Left Brigade – Relief complete 7 PM – On relief Coys of the 13th R.W.Fus. took up their [illegible] on CANAL BANK EAST.	
	" 13th "	—	[illegible] – The 13th Bn R.W.Fus. relieved by the 15th Bn Welsh Regt. in the ~~Left~~ Right Support [illegible] – The 13th R.W.Fus. relieved the 15th Bn R.W.Fus. in the Left Support of the Right Brigade – Relief complete – 11 PM	

2353 Wt. W2544/1454 700,000 5/15 D. D. & L. A.D.S.S./Forms/C. 2118.

Instructions regarding War Diaries and Intelligence Summaries are contained in F. S. Regs., Part II. and the Staff Manual respectively. Title pages will be prepared in manuscript.

WAR DIARY
or
INTELLIGENCE SUMMARY.
(*Erase heading not required.*)

Army Form C. 2118.

Place	Date	Hour	Summary of Events and Information	Remarks and references to Appendices
In the field	MARCH 11th	----	Increased artillery activity on the front. Visibility very good. Considerable aerial activity from 9 A.M. to 5 P.M. - Frequent aerial engagements took place during which two 'planes were observed falling. reported to have been ours.	S. H. [illegible] Major Commanding 13th Bn. R.W. Fusrs.
" " "	12-3-17	----	Hostile artillery very active very active during the afternoon mostly directed on to the CANAL BANK and our batteries - Our artillery retaliated heavily during the night on enemy's back areas.	
" " "	13-3-17	----	No artillery activity on the front. - Enemy machine guns active during the night.	
" " "	14-3-17	----	Very little artillery activity on the front. - The 13th Bn. R.W. Fus relieved the 16th Bn. R.W. Fus. in the Left Subsection of the Right Brigade - relief complete 7-55 P.M. - On relief Coys. of the 13th R.W. Fus. took up the following dispositions - "A" Coy - RIGHT FRONT. - "B" Coy. - RIGHT SUPPORT. - "C" Coy - LEFT FRONT "D" Coy - LEFT SUPPORT.	
" " "	15-3-17	----	Enemy artillery very active on our back areas between 10 A.M. & 12 noon. - Several heavy shrapnel fired on to CANAL BANK in the neighbourhood of BRIDGE 6. - During the afternoon enemy fired approximately 400 heavy shells on one of our batteries.	
" " "	16-3-17	----	From 9 - 11 A.M. hostile artillery was fairly active on our back areas. - Remainder of the day very quiet. During the night hostile machine guns were not so active - About 9-15 P.M. enemy fired a few shells on to our support lines.	
" " "	17-3-17	----	At 3-15 A.M. our artillery fired a few shells on to enemy's front line. - Considerable aerial activity throughout the day.	
" " "	18-3-17	----	Very little activity on the front during the morning. - Our artillery fired continuously on enemy's back areas during the afternoon. - The 13th Bn. R.W. Fusrs. relieved by the 16th Bn. R.W. Fus. in the Left Subsection of the Right Brigade. - relief complete 7-55 P.M. On relief Coys. of the 13th R.W. Fus took up their positions on CANAL BANK E. - LEFT SUPPORT.	
" " "	19-3-17	----	Very quiet day - Considerable machine gun fire during the night.	
" " "	20-3-17	----	No artillery activity during the day - Enemy machine guns very active from 9 - 11 P.M. - An unusual number of "very lights" sent up from enemy's lines during the night.	

2353 Wt. W2544/1454 700,000 5/15 D. D. & L. A.D.S.S./Forms/C. 2118.

Instructions regarding War Diaries and Intelligence Summaries are contained in F. S. Regs., Part II. and the Staff Manual respectively. Title pages will be prepared in manuscript.

WAR DIARY
or
INTELLIGENCE SUMMARY.
(Erase heading not required.)

Army Form C. 2118.

Place	Date	Hour	Summary of Events and Information	Remarks and references to Appendices
In the field	21-3-17		Considerable artillery activity - Enemy fired continuously on to our batteries and back areas - Our artillery retaliated heavily on enemy's front line between 4-6 P.M. - The 13th Bn. R.W. Fus relieved by the 10th Bn S.W.B in the Left Support of the Right Brigade - relief complete - 10-20 P.M. - On completion of relief 13th Bn R.W. Fus marched to YPRES ASYLUM station, entraining for BOLLEZEELE at 11-30 P.M.	
	22-3-17		13th R.W. Fus arrived ESQUELBECQ STATION 4-30 A.M. - BREAKFASTS around 5 A.M. - At 6 A.M. the Battalion proceeded to BOLLEZEELE arriving at [illegible] A.M. - Remainder of the day spent in cleaning up	
	23-3-17	9 A.M. - 12-30	[illegible] battled	
		2-30 P.M. - 3-45	Training around billets	
	24-3-17	9 A.M.	13th R.W. Fus proceeded to TRAINING AREA - G.3 & 5 where training was carried out until 12-30 P.M. - From 2-30 P.M. - 4 P.M. Coys went through a programme of training in the field at A 23. b [illegible] - Recreational training from 5 - 6 P.M.	
	25-3-17		Training around billets - Recreational training from 3 - 5 P.M.	
	26-3-17		Training on area G 3 & 5 from 9 A.M. - 3-45 P.M. - dinners in the field	
	27-3-17		Training on area G 3 & 5 from 9 A.M. - 3-45 P.M. - dinners in the field - Recreational training from 5 - 6 P.M.	
	28-3-17		Training on area G 3 & 5 from 9 A.M. - 3-45 P.M. - dinners in the field - Recreational training from 5 - 6 P.M.	
	29-3-17		Training on area G 3 & 5 from 9 A.M. - 3-45 P.M. - [illegible] tactical scheme carried out from 8 - 11 P.M.	
	30-3-17		Training around billets during the morning - Recreational training from 3 - 5 P.M.	
	31-3-17		13th Bn R.W. Fus marched to ESQUELBECQ entraining at 6 P.M. for YPRES ASYLUM station - On arrival Batt marched to [illegible] relieving the 13th Bn Welsh Regt. in the Left Support of the Right Brigade.	
	1-4-17		[illegible] activity on the front - 13th Bn R.W. Fusrs relieved the 10th Bn Welsh Regiment in the Left Subsection of the Right Brigade - Relief complete - 9-45 P.M.	

E. Lance Kelly Major
Commanding 13th R.W. Fusrs.

2353 Wt. W2544/1454 700,000 5/15 D. D. & L. A.D.S.S./Forms/C 2118.

13th BATTN. ROYAL WELSH FUSILIERS Vol 17

WAR DIARY

FOR

APRIL 1917

17.B.
[illegible]

Army Form C. 2118.

WAR DIARY
or
INTELLIGENCE SUMMARY.
(Erase heading not required.)

Instructions regarding War Diaries and Intelligence Summaries are contained in F. S. Regs., Part II. and the Staff Manual respectively. Title pages will be prepared in manuscript.

Place	Date	Hour	Summary of Events and Information	Remarks and references to Appendices
In the field.	1-4-17.	......	Enemy [illegible] artillery registered on several points on our front particularly SKIPTON and THE PILE also BUFFS [illegible]. The junction of [illegible] DRAIN EAST [illegible] also received attention. Our heavy artillery did a good deal of firing on enemy's front and support lines, also back areas. Hostile machine guns were very active during the night.	R D [illegible] Lt. Col. Commanding 13th Bn. R.W. Fus.
" " " " "	2-4-17	......	No artillery or Trench Mortar activity on our front line. Hostile artillery fired intermittently on our back area during the day. Marked aerial activity on both sides between [illegible] and [illegible] – [illegible] observed falling [illegible] the [illegible] SECTOR about [illegible] A.M. – reported to have been enemy's. Our artillery fired at intervals on selected targets in enemy's front and support lines during the day. At [illegible] P.M. enemy artillery shelled LANCASHIRE FARM & [illegible]. Our artillery retaliated heavily.	
" " " " "	3-4-17	......	Quiet during the morning. At [illegible] P.M. enemy fired four Light Trench Mortars into [illegible] causing no damage. [illegible] our medium Trench Mortar Battery retaliated. Between [illegible] and 5-15 P.M. enemy fired a heavy shrapnel shells bursting between our front line and LANCASHIRE FARM. Considerable aerial activity between 5-30 & 6-30 P.M. Hostile machine guns very active from [illegible] to [illegible] P.M. traversing near LANCASHIRE FARM.	
" " " " "	4-4-17	......	Hostile artillery very quiet throughout the day. Our artillery was fairly active on enemy's back areas. The 11th Bn. R.W. Fus. relieved by the 13th Bn. R.W. Fus. in the left subsection of the Right Brigade. Relief complete [illegible] P.M. On completion of relief Coys. of the 13th Bn. R.W. Fusrs. took up their positions in CANAL BANK EAST & left support.	
" " " " "	5-4-17	......	[illegible] [illegible] P.M. when enemy shelled LANCASHIRE FARM and surrounding trenches. Heavy bombardment [illegible] during the night. Our artillery quieter than usual.	
" " " " "	6-4-17	......	At [illegible] P.M. our artillery shelled enemy trenches in the vicinity of KRUPP FARM. Smoke seen issuing from enemy's lines at approximately C.11.a.5.4. At [illegible] P.M. few of the enemy were seen [illegible] a gap in the front line at C.19.a.3.4. Hostile shelling [illegible] Hostile Machine Guns very active during the night.	
" " " " "	7-4-17	......	[illegible] aerial activity during the early morning ([illegible]). Artillery on both sides quiet. At [illegible] P.M. approximately an intense bombardment opened on the right lasting until [illegible] midnight. Numerous [illegible] of [illegible] [illegible] Burning. The [illegible] and [illegible] aeroplanes were active [illegible] [illegible] about 9 P.M.	
" " " " "	8-4-17.	......	Visibility good and artillery on both sides active until 5 P.M. The 13th Bn. R.W. Fusrs. relieved the 11th Bn. R.W. Fusrs. in the left subsection of the Right Brigade. Relief complete [illegible] 9-15 P.M. On completion of relief Coys. of the 13th R.W. Fus. took up the following dispositions. "A" Coy. – RIGHT FRONT. "B" Coy. – RIGHT SUPPORT. "C" Coy. – LEFT FRONT. "D" Coy. – LEFT SUPPORT.	

£353 Wt. W2544/1454 700,000 5/15 D. D. & L. A.D.S.S./Forms/C. 2118.

Army Form C. 2118.

Instructions regarding War Diaries and Intelligence Summaries are contained in F. S. Regs., Part II. and the Staff Manual respectively. Title pages will be prepared in manuscript.

WAR DIARY
or
INTELLIGENCE SUMMARY.

(Erase heading not required.)

Place	Date	Hour	Summary of Events and Information	Remarks and references to Appendices
In the field.	9-4-17.		Very quiet along the front. – At 6 P.M. enemy artillery commenced firing on BRIELEN and AUSTERLITZ. – A considerable number of rounds were fired but no damage done – Considerable machine gun and rifle fire during the night. – In retaliation our Lewis Guns were active. – Enemy appeared to be very nervous and the least noise from our lines produced considerable machine gun fire.	[signature] Lt: Col. Commanding 13th Bn. R.W. Fusrs.
" " "	10-4-17.		At 2-15 A.M. enemy seemed to be alarmed and opened intense machine gun fire, sent up numerous "very" lights and bombed his own wire. – Artillery activity on both sides practically NIL. – Enemy machine guns not so active as previous nights. 'B' Coy. 13th R.W. Fus. relieved 'A' Coy. – RIGHT FRONT. 'D' Coy. relieved 'C' Coy. – LEFT FRONT – relief complete – 4 P.M.	
" " "	11-4-17.		Quiet along the whole front. – The 13th Bn. R.W. Fus. relieved by the 10th Bn. Welsh Regiment as Relief in the Left Subsection of the Right Brigade – Relief complete 12 midnight. On relief 13th Bn. R.W. Fus. marched to 'D' Camp.	
" " "	12-4-17.		Kits inspected and men bathed. 2nd Lieut. W. A. Martin & 2nd Lieut. P. Lunt rejoined the Battalion. – Lt. G. M. Jones resumed duties as Adjutant	
" " "	13-4-17.		Training in 'D' Camp.	
" " "	14-4-17.		Training in 'D' Camp.	
" " "	15-4-17.		Training in 'D' Camp.	
" " "	16-4-17.		Training in 'D' Camp. – 3 officers joined the Battalion – 2nd Lieut. R. Williams, 2nd Lieut. G. Holt, 2nd Lieut. E. Fletcher.	
" " "	17-4-17.		Training in 'D' Camp.	
" " "	18-4-17.		Training in 'D' Camp. – Gas demonstration carried out and all helmets tested.	
" " "	19-4-17.		Training in 'D' Camp. –	
" " "	20-4-17.		Training in 'D' Camp.	
" " "	21-4-17.		Training in 'D' Camp.	
" " "	22-4-17.		Training during the morning. – The 13th Bn. R.W. Fus. started from 'D' Camp at 8-30 P.M. & relieved the 15th Bn. the Welsh Regiment in the ~~Left~~ Right Support of the Right Brigade – relief complete 11-30 P.M.	
" " "	23-4-17.		Considerable aerial activity on both sides. – Enemy fired a few shells on FOCH FARM about 11 A.M. No hostile shelling on our front line during the morning – From 1 to 2 P.M. a few shells were fired on to our front line at various points	
" " "	24-4-17.		Our artillery very active throughout the day – Shells observed falling on enemy's wire and at front line at KRUPP SALIENT. – In retaliation enemy sent a few trench mortars on to our front line – no damage done.	

Army Form C. 2118.

Instructions regarding War Diaries and Intelligence Summaries are contained in F. S. Regs., Part II. and the Staff Manual respectively. Title pages will be prepared in manuscript.

WAR DIARY
or
INTELLIGENCE SUMMARY.
(Erase heading not required.)

Place	Date	Hour	Summary of Events and Information	Remarks and references to Appendices
In the field	24-4-17 (continued)		At 10 P.M. enemy opened a heavy bombardment on the right which spread along our front. Our artillery retaliated heavily. All quiet by 10-45 P.M. Considerable aerial activity on both sides.	[signature] Lt. Col. Commanding 13th Bn. R.W. Fusrs.
" " "	25-4-17		Our artillery shelled at intervals all morning firing on enemy's wire and front line. Enemy sent over a few Trench Mortars between 5-30 & 1 P.M. Visibility very good during the afternoon.	
" " "	26-4-17		Considerable aerial activity. Our aeroplanes patrolled enemy's lines in large numbers between 5 & 8 P.M. Hostile planes driven off. Very little hostile shelling on the front. Our batteries fired frequent bursts on enemy's wire. The 13th Bn. R.W. Fusrs. relieved the 16th Bn. R.W. Fusrs. in the Right Sub-section of the Right Brigade. Relief complete 10-50 P.M. Coys. of the 13th Bn. R.W. Fus took up the following dispositions. 'B' Coy. right front. 'A' Coy. right support. 'D' Coy. Left Front. 'C' Coy. Left Support.	
" " "	27-4-17		Our artillery in conjunction with Medium Trench Mortars fired on enemy's wire and front line from 11 A.M. 3-30 p.m. Two or three of our Trench Mortar bombs dropped short on our front line by FUSILIER TRENCH. Enemy replied with two "MINNIES" causing no damage. Enemy very quiet.	
" " "	28-4-17		Our artillery bombarded selected points in enemy line from KRUPP CORNER to VON KLUCK'S COPSE. Enemy's retaliation was feeble. At 2-55 P.M. a few light shells were fired on to the HILL, LANCS. FARM, SKIPTON TERRACE – little damage done. [illegible] ROAD also [illegible]	
" " "	29-4-17		From 11 A.M. to 1 P.M. heavy artillery bombardment of selected points in enemy lines and back areas. Direct hits observed on [illegible] [illegible] enemy artillery fired H.E. & shrapnel on the HILL, SKIPTON, HEADINGLEY TERRACE FARM. 1-10 – 2-20 P.M. [illegible] At 9-30 P.M. 'D' Coy. 13th R.W.F. carried out a "dummy raid". An intense bombardment of enemy's lines from 9-30 P.M. to 10 P.M. Enemy's retaliation confined chiefly to our support lines.	
" "	30-4-17		At 12-30 A.M. a raiding party successfully raided enemy trenches (MORTELDJE SALIENT) under cover of an intense bombardment by our artillery. Enemy retaliated heavily on our front & support lines but no considerable damage done. The remainder of the day fairly quiet. 13th relieved by 16th R.W.F. Relief complete. 9.40 pm.	

2353 Wt. W2544/1454 700,000 5/15 D. D. & L. A.D.S.S./Forms/C. 2118.

Vol 18

13th ROYAL WELSH FUSILIERS

WAR DIARY

FOR

MAY 1917

18 B.
4 sheets

WAR DIARY
or
INTELLIGENCE SUMMARY.
(Erase heading not required.)

Army Form C. 2118.

Instructions regarding War Diaries and Intelligence Summaries are contained in F. S. Regs., Part II. and the Staff Manual respectively. Title pages will be prepared in manuscript.

Place	Date	Hour	Summary of Events and Information	Remarks and references to Appendices
[illegible]	[illegible]		[illegible]	

Instructions regarding War Diaries and Intelligence Summaries are contained in F. S. Regs., Part II. and the Staff Manual respectively. Title Pages will be prepared in manuscript.

WAR DIARY
or
INTELLIGENCE SUMMARY
(Erase heading not required.)

Army Form C. 2118

Place	Date	Hour	Summary of Events and Information	Remarks and references to Appendices
In the field	12-5-17.		From 6-45 to 8 AM. hostile artillery fired a few 77mm. shells on HUDDERSFIELD, SKIPTON, THE NILE and LANCASHIRE FARM. At 6-45 P.M. fired a few rifle grenades on to the front line. - At 1 P.M. our heavies fired on back areas. - Day quiet on the whole. - 13th Bn. R.W. Fusrs. relieved 11th Bn. R.W. Fusrs. in the Right Subsection of the Right Brigade - relief complete 8-45 P.M.	
" " "	13-5-17.		Between 6 & 8 A.M. enemy sent over some light Trench Mortar bombs on to our front line, also a few pineapples on FUSILIER FARM. - 9-30 A.M. CAVAN DRAIN & HUDDERSFIELD lightly shelled. - From 6 to 8 P.M. enemy batteries fired a considerable number of rounds on to our back areas. - Our stokes retaliated for hostile trench mortars at 6-30 A.M. Our heavy artillery fired on back areas during the afternoon. - About 1-45 P.M. a Belgian Observation Balloon was attacked by a hostile 'plane and seen falling in flames.	
" " "	14-5-17		At 2-57 A.M. enemy opened an intense bombardment on our front and support lines, - the front line being subjected to very heavy trench mortar fire. - Shortly after the commencement of hostile bombardment a party of the enemy numbering about 40 were observed by POSTS 21 and POST 22 advancing in small parties across NO MAN'S LAND towards C.14.10. - Our posts immediately opened rapid fire, and the Lewis Guns in POSTS 21 & 22 brought enfilade fire to bear upon the enemy, causing casualties and the withdrawal of the raiding party. - One wounded prisoner brought in from our wire. Our artillery, trench mortar batteries, and stokes all opened fire very soon after the commencement of hostile bombardment and kept it up until hostile fire had ceased. Situation normal at 3-50 A.M.	
" " "			During the remainder of the day hostile activity confined chiefly to our back areas. - Our artillery fired intermittently throughout the day.	
" " "	15-5-17		Quiet day. - Very little activity on forward areas - our artillery fire confined mainly to enemy back areas. - Aerial activity very marked.	
" " "	16-5-17		Very quiet day - nothing unusual to report on our front. - Visibility low. - 13th Bn. R.W. Fusrs. relieved by the 11th Bn. R.W. Fusrs. in the Right Subsection of the Right Brigade - relief complete 8-50 P.M. - On completion of relief Coys. of 13th R.W. Fus. took up their positions on CANAL BANK E. - RIGHT SUPPORT.	
" " "	17-5-17		Our artillery fired intermittently during the day. - Visibility low - a heavy mist prevailing. - No hostile activity on the front.	
" " "	18-5-17		Hostile 'plane patrolled our lines between 8 & 11 A.M. - forced to withdraw eventually by our Anti-aircraft guns. 13th Bn. R.W. Fus. relieved by the 15th Bn. Welch Regiment in the Right Support - relief complete [illegible] P.M. On relief 13th R.W. Fus marched to the ASYLUM, YPRES, entraining for POPERINGHE at 12 midnight. - [illegible]	R. Campbell Lt. Col. Commanding 13th Bn. R.W. Fusrs.

1875 Wt. W593/826 1,000,000 4/15 J.B.C. & A. A.D.S.S./Forms/C. 2118.

Army Form C. 2118

Instructions regarding War Diaries and Intelligence Summaries are contained in F. S. Regs., Part II. and the Staff Manual respectively. Title Pages will be prepared in manuscript.

WAR DIARY

or

INTELLIGENCE SUMMARY

(Erase heading not required.)

Place	Date	Hour	Summary of Events and Information	Remarks and references to Appendices
[illegible]	[illegible]		[illegible]	[illegible]

1875 Wt. W593/826 1,000,000 4/15 J.B.C. & A. A.D.S.S./Forms/C. 2118.

Vol 19

13th BATT. ROYAL WELSH FUSILIERS

WAR DIARY

FOR

JUNE 1917

19.B
5 sheets

Instructions regarding War Diaries and Intelligence Summaries are contained in F. S. Regs., Part II and the Staff Manual respectively. Title pages will be prepared in manuscript.

WAR DIARY
or
INTELLIGENCE SUMMARY.
(Erase heading not required.)

Army Form C. 2118.

Place	Date	Hour	Summary of Events and Information	Remarks and references to Appendices
In the Field	1-6-17.	—	Training.	
" " "	2-6-17.	—	Training.	
" " "	3-6-17	—	Training.	
" " "	4-6-17	—	Training.	
" " "	5-6-17.	—	Training.	
" " "	6-6-17	—	Training.	
" " "	7-6-17	—	Training.	
" " "	8-6-17.	—	Training.	
" " "	9-6-17	—	Training.	
" " "	10-6-17	—	13th Bn R.W. Fusrs. left the QUELMES AREA at 8·30 A.M., entraining at ST. OMER for POPERINGHE - at 11 A.M. Arrived POPERINGHE Train and marched to "L" Camp.	
" " "	11-6-17	—	13th Bn R.W. Fusrs. entrained at POPERINGHE at 10 P.M. for CANAL BANK, detraining at H.10.b.5.1. The Battalion then marched to CANAL BANK relieving the 15th Bn. Welch Regiment, in the Right support to the Right Brigade - [illegible] Relief complete 1 A.M.	
" " "	12-6-17.		The 13th Bn R.W. Fus. relieved the 10th Bn. The Welch Regiment in the Right Subsection of the Right Brigade - relief complete 7·45 P.M.	

2351 Wt. W2541/1454 700,000 5/15 D. D. & L. A.D.S.S./Forms/C. 2118.

Instructions regarding War Diaries and Intelligence Summaries are contained in F. S. Regs., Part II. and the Staff Manual respectively. Title pages will be prepared in manuscript.

WAR DIARY
or
INTELLIGENCE SUMMARY.
(Erase heading not required.)

Army Form C. 2118.

Place	Date	Hour	Summary of Events and Information	Remarks and references to Appendices
In the field	12-6-17.		Between 9 P.M. & 12 midnight enemy shelled our support and back areas	R O Campbell Lt. Col. 13th R W Fus.
" " "	13-6-17.		At 2-50 A.M. several shells were fired on LANCASHIRE FARM. and again at 3 a.m. - The remainder of the day very quiet - a few shells were fired on our support line - Our artillery was fairly quiet during the day.	
" "	14-6-17.		At 3-15 am SKIPTON + LANCASHIRE FM heavily shelled for 25 minutes. 8-30 - 9 am HUDDERSFIELD + CAVAN DN shelled. During the evening CANALBANK was heavily shelled with 4.2 + 5.9 shells	
	15/6/17		CAVAN DRAIN shelled at following times 8-30 - 9.15; 10-10 - 12-5. Concussions of the earth felt twice at 11-30 pm + 11.48.	
	16/6/17		Enemy Arty active all day firing steadily. Three planes over Canal Bank & two over YPRES. Situation normal	
	17/6/17		Enemy quiet yesterday except intermittent shelling through day.. 2 planes flying low at 2-30 am	
	18/6/17	1.20 AM 1.30 AM	Considerable hostile shelling during the day - especially from 1.20 AM to 1.30 AM the shelling was heavy on CAVAN DRAIN and HUDDERSFIELD TRENCH. - Our Artillery continued to shell enemy's back areas with heavies.	
		9.55 PM.	Enemy dropped 10 cm shells in the vicinity of BRIDGES - CANAL BANK WEST and from then on through the night he continued to shell CANAL BANK and roads to BRAKLEN.	

Instructions regarding War Diaries and Intelligence Summaries are contained in F. S. Regs., Part II. and the Staff Manual respectively. Title pages will be prepared in manuscript.

WAR DIARY
or
INTELLIGENCE SUMMARY.

(Erase heading not required.)

Army Form C. 2118.

Place	Date	Hour	Summary of Events and Information	Remarks and references to Appendices
In the field. NILE SUBSECTION.	19/VI/17.	12.30AM 1.10AM.	Enemy shelled SKIPTON and FRONT LINE with 10.5 cm and 77 mm — light shelling. Later CAVAN DRAIN, EALING, BULLY, SKIPTON C.T. and FRONT LINE. During the time he put up various coloured lights. From 2.0 AM intermittent shelling of LANCASHIRE FARM and HUDDERSFIELD C.T. until 4.0 AM. when hostile plane came over our lines — Our Artillery continued shelling back areas.	R. W. Campbell [illegible] 13th R. W. Fus.
		4.45pm	Enemy front line [illegible] fired on. Various coloured lights sent up between [illegible] and [illegible]. Golden rain bursting into 2 [illegible] others bursting into 2 reds. Two hostile planes flying very low over our lines. [illegible]	
	20/VI/17.	8.0 pm 1.0 AM	[illegible] intermittently. A few Golden rain rockets — nothing apparently followed. There seemed to be less Very lights sent up over front than on other fronts. Enemy very quiet during the night.	
		6 pm 6.15pm 9.30pm	Enemy [illegible] front of CAVAN DRAIN. The [illegible] of [illegible] and [illegible] FARM were shelled.	
	21/VI/17.	[illegible] AM	Enemy plane brought down. During the night enemy sent up Golden rain rockets from front and support line. CAVAN DRAIN shelled intermittently. — Inter-company relief. A minor [illegible] took place on our left — 15th Bn. R. W. Fus. — During this time enemy M.G. fire on our front was very intense. Two red lights were apparently the S.O.S. signal on our left. These were sent up [illegible] the operation was in progress.	
	22/VI/17.	12.30pm 12.45pm	The enemy was quiet during the greater part of the day. Enemy shelled RAILWAY nearly B.30.b.30.25, NILE and later on SKIPTON with 10.5 cm shells.	
		7.15 " 7.50 – 10 pm	Shelling was repeated on above points. — Inter-company relief. CANAL BANK and roadway around C.19.c.50.00 shelled with 10.5 cm shells — [illegible] continued shelling of back areas.	
	23/VI/17.	12.35AM 1.0 AM.	CAVAN DRAIN shelled with 10.5 cm shells.	
		3.0 AM 5.0pm	Front line shelled [about C [illegible]] with 77 mm. CANAL BANK shelled in vicinity Bridge 6B with 10.5 cms shells — Hostile aeroplane heavily shelled by our A.A. guns, and driven off. Two planes attacked one of our machines but was driven off by M.G. fire.	
	24/VI/17.	1 AM	Enemy M.G.'s active at intervals during the night. The NILE received considerable attention [illegible] — the enemy shelling it with [illegible] shells — [illegible] fired on [illegible] [illegible] CANAL BANKS E & W from [illegible] 20.00 to C.13.a.20.70 [illegible] shelled lightly — concentration being made on bridges.	
		12 NOON	Large number of [illegible] were [illegible] (nearly [illegible]).	
		11.30pm	Minor Enterprise by 13th Bn. R. W. Fus. attempted. 4 officers and 93 O.R. attempted to enter the enemy trench at C.[illegible].35.35. but could not penetrate the enemy wire which appeared to be in three belts. The first and second belts were damaged and trampled down in parts, and consisted of concertina wiring and knife rests. There was no [illegible], and a dip in the ground, found running parallel to enemy parapet, filled with thick barbed concertina and broken knife rests, which was continued up to the parapet. The enemy post at C.[illegible].35.35. was occupied — Casualties 1 man wounded.	
		[illegible] pm [illegible] pm	Intercompany relief in NILE SUBSECTION. [13th Bn. R. W. Fus.]	

2353 Wt. W2544/1454 700,000 5/15 D. D. & L. A.D.S.S. Forms/C. 2118.

Instructions regarding War Diaries and Intelligence Summaries are contained in F. S. Regs., Part II. and the Staff Manual respectively. Title pages will be prepared in manuscript.

WAR DIARY
or
INTELLIGENCE SUMMARY.
(Erase heading not required.)

Army Form C. 2118.

Place	Date	Hour	Summary of Events and Information	Remarks and references to Appendices
In the field. [N.I.F.] RIGHT SUBSECTION.	25/VI/17	2.30AM. 3.0AM. 3.30AM.	Bridges 6 to 6W. heavily shelled with 15 cm and 10.5 cm shells – later at 3.0AM Bridges 6B – 6W heavily shelled. During this time all C.T.'s were heavily barraged.	Letters C.B. used meaning – CANAL BANK.
		4.0AM 4.15AM	The above operation repeated – and intermittently throughout the day these points were shelled – two 10.5 cm and one 15 cm. gun being used by the enemy.	
			Enemy sent up coloured rockets (orange colour) when his artillery fired on his own front line.	
	26/VI/17	10.0 AM 1.PM.	CANAL BANK shelled intermittently between Bridges 4 and 6.	
		11.0AM	H.R.H. the PRINCE OF WALES visited 13th Bn. R.W. Fus HQ.	
		5.0 pm 7.0 pm	Intercompany relief – Very much decreased shelling of CANAL BANK. 11th Bn. R.W. Fus. raided carried out a raid (Pond Bank?) without success.	
	27/VI/17	12 MN.	Enemy unusually quiet – absence of usual shelling of C.B. and road YPRES – BOESINGHE.	
			An occasional shell dropping bursting on various points.	
		11.0AM 1.0PM	Heavy shelling of CANAL BANK in vicinity of BRIDGE 4 – Enemy probably aiming at the Bridge –	
		3.15pm 5.30pm	Very little aeroplane activity on our part – Several German planes over the line during the day. One of our balloons was brought down in flames by a hostile plane, another balloon was also brought down	
		10.0 PM 12.0 MN	Absence of shelling – Transport able to bring up rations without being shelled.	
	28/VI/17	1.48AM	B & D companies 13th Bn. R.W. Fus relieved in support between BRIDGES 4 & 5 C.B. E. by 2 companies 1st Bn. ROYAL INNISKILLING FUS. – relief complete 1.48 A.M. – Night quiet –	
		7.15P.M.	A & C Coys. 13th. Bn. R.W. Fus. relieved in front line by 2 companies (in support) 1st. Bn. R. Inniskilling Fus.	⊗
	29/VI/17.	12.30AM	⊗ Relief of 2 companies & Bn HQ complete. —— Battalion in bivouac at Transport Lines.	
		9.0AM.	13th. Bn. R.W. Fus. entrained – arrived in camp at EECRNEEST at 1.30p.m. (S.W. of CAESTRE.)	
	30/VI/17.	7.0AM	Battalion marched to HAZEBROUCK, and entrained arriving in billets 10.30AM. at LIGNY-LES-AIRES.	

R.D. Campbell Lt Col
13th RW Fus

2353 Wt. W2544/1454 700,000 5/15 D. D. & L. A.D.S.S. Forms/C. 2118.

Vol 20

13th Bn Royal Welsh Fusiliers

113/38

War Diary

July - 1917

Instructions regarding War Diaries and Intelligence Summaries are contained in F. S. Regs., Part II. and the Staff Manual respectively. Title pages will be prepared in manuscript.

WAR DIARY
or
INTELLIGENCE SUMMARY.
(Erase heading not required.)

Army Form C. 2118.

Place	Date	Hour	Summary of Events and Information	Remarks and references to Appendices
In the field	1-7-17		13th Bn. R.W.Fus. billetted at LIGNY-lez-AIRE	
" "	2-7-17		Training carried out by Companies around billets.	
" "	3-7-17		Field Day on SPECIAL MANOEUVRE AREA allotted to the 38th (Welsh) Division at ENGUINEGATTE - Reference Map - THÉROUANNE - SHEET 36a R23 & R24	
" "	4-7-17		Field Day on SPECIAL MANOEUVRE AREA allotted to the 38th (Welsh) Division at ENGUINEGATTE - Reference Map - THÉROUANNE SHEET 36a R23 & R24	
" "	5-7-17		Field Day on SPECIAL MANOEUVRE AREA allotted to the 38th (Welsh) Division at ENGUINEGATTE - Reference Map - THÉROUANNE - SHEET 36a - R23 & R24.	
" "	6-7-17		Field Day on SPECIAL MANOEUVRE AREA allotted to the 38th (Welsh) Division at ENGUINEGATTE - Reference Map - THÉROUANNE - SHEET 36a - R23 & R. 24	
" "	7-7-17		Field Day on SPECIAL MANOEUVRE AREA allotted to the 38th (Welsh) Division at ENGUINEGATTE - Reference Map - THÉROUANNE - SHEET 36a - R23 & R. 24	
" "	8-7-17		Voluntary Church Services - No Parades	
" "	9-7-17		Brigade Field Day on SPECIAL MANOEUVRE AREA allotted to the 38th (Welsh) Division at ENGUINEGATTE - Reference Map - THÉROUANNE - SHEET 36a. R23 & R.24	
" "	10-7-17		Field Day on SPECIAL MANOEUVRE AREA allotted to the 38th (Welsh) Division at ENGUINEGATTE - Reference Map - THÉROUANNE - SHEET 36a - R23 & R.24	
" "	11-7-17		Field Day on SPECIAL MANOEUVRE AREA allotted to the 38th (Welsh) Division at ENGUINEGATTE - Reference Map - THÉROUANNE - SHEET 36a - R23 & R 24	
" "	12-7-17		Divisional Field Day on SPECIAL MANOEUVRE AREA allotted to the 38th (Welsh) Division at ENGUINEGATTE - Reference Map - THÉROUANNE - SHEET 36a R.23 & R 24	

[illegible]
Major
13th Bn. Royal Welsh Fusiliers.

Instructions regarding War Diaries and Intelligence Summaries are contained in F. S. Regs., Part II. and the Staff Manual respectively. Title pages will be prepared in manuscript.

WAR DIARY
or
INTELLIGENCE SUMMARY.

(Erase heading not required.)

Army Form C. 2118.

Place	Date	Hour	Summary of Events and Information	Remarks and references to Appendices
In the field	13-7-17		Inspection of Billets etc - No parades.	Major. 13th Bn. R.W. Fusrs.
" " "	14-7-17		Training by Companies in SPECIAL MANOEUVRE AREA allotted to 38th (Welsh) Division at ENGUINEGATTE - Reference Map - THÉROUANNE - SHEET 36a R.4 & R.24.	
" " "	15-7-17		Company Training during morning around billets - Voluntary Church Services during afternoon.	
" " "	16-7-17		13th Bn. R.W. Fusrs. left LIGNY-LES-AIRE at 5 AM and marched to STEENBECQUE arriving 1.50 P.M.	
" " "	17-7-17		13th Bn. R.W. Fusrs. left STEENBECQUE at 6.30 AM and marched to the HONDEGHEM AREA arriving at 11 AM.	
" " "	18-7-17		13th Bn. R.W. Fusrs. left HONDEGHEM AREA at 5.15 AM for camp near HOUTKERQUE - Reference Map - ~~[illegible]~~ SHEET 27 N.E. E.16.a.9.5. - arriving at 9.00 AM	
" " "	19-7-17		13th Bn. R.W. Fusrs. left Camp at E.16.a.9.5 at 7.15 AM and marched to camp at F.5.C. - Reference Map - SHEET 27 N.E.	
" " "	20-7-17		Company Training until noon.	
" " "	21-7-17		13th Bn. R.W. Fusrs. left camp at F.5.C. and marched to H. Camp. arriving at 12 noon.	
" " "	22-7-17		Voluntary Church services. - No parades.	
" " "	23-7-17		Company Training.	
" " "	24-7-17	P.M. 9.10.	13th Bn. R.W. Fus. marched from H Camp [F.5.C.] to the ZWAANHOF SECTOR - via tracks 9 & 10 - to relieve 14th Bn. R.W. Fus. in the front line - the enemy sent over several gas shells on CANAL BANK W. between bridges 6 and 6 W. - also on front line - this hindered the relief considerably.	

2353 Wt. W2544/1454 700,000 5/15 D. D. & L. A.D.S.S. Forms/C 2118.

Army Form C. 2118.

Instructions regarding War Diaries and Intelligence Summaries are contained in F. S. Regs., Part II. and the Staff Manual respectively. Title pages will be prepared in manuscript.

WAR DIARY
or
INTELLIGENCE SUMMARY.
(Erase heading not required.)

Place	Date	Hour	Summary of Events and Information	Remarks and references to Appendices
In the field	25/vii/17	1.50 AM.	13th Bn. R.W. Fus relieved 14th. Bn. R.W.Fus. — relief complete.	
		4.0 AM	Gas was detected in HARVEY TRENCH — CAPT. DEBUS became a casualty due to gas — 2/LTS FLETCHER	
" " " "			and BANYARD were wounded — not seriously — by shrapnel.	
			On the whole the enemy was much quieter — his artillery firing but very little.	
" " " "		10.0 AM	Raiding Party of 15th Bn. R.W. Fus. — under cover of the Practice Barrage and a Box Barrage — entered the enemy	
			trenches between C.7.c., 80.75. to C.7.d., 50.60. which they found unoccupied, and failed to	
" " " "			find identification. — One officer and one O.R. reported missing.	
	26/vii/17.		Enemy artillery fire below normal — slight Gas shelling around ESSEX TRENCH	
			during the evening — Our artillery bombarded enemy lines throughout the day.	
			Our heavies fired on back areas at intervals during the night —	
			13th. Bn. R.W. Fus. relieved by 15th. Bn. R.W. Fus. in front line — relief complete	
			7.30 pm. Upon relief 13th Bn. R.W. Fus. went into support on CANAL BANK. W.	
			and were relieved by 10th. Bn. Rifle Brigade — relief complete 11.30 pm. —	
			13th Bn. R.W. Fus. marched to camp at A.10.c., 5.6. (sheet 28.N.W.) bivouacs	
" " " "	27/vii/17.		13th Bn. R.W. Fusrs. bivouacked in camp at A.10.c.5.6. (Sheet. 28 N.W.).	
" " " "	28/vii/17.		13th Bn. R.W. Fusrs. bivouacked in camp at A.10.c.5.6. (Sheet 28 N.W).	
" " " "	29/vii/17.		13th Bn. R.W. Fusrs. left camp at 6-30. P.M. & relieved 10th Bn. Rifle Brigade in reserve on CANAL BANK — Relief complete 10 P.M.	[signature] Major. 13th Bn. R.W. Fusrs.

2353 Wt. W2544/1454 700,000 5/15 D. D. & L. A.D.S.S. Forms/C 2118.

Instructions regarding War Diaries and Intelligence Summaries are contained in F. S. Regs., Part II. and the Staff Manual respectively. Title pages will be prepared in manuscript.

WAR DIARY
or
INTELLIGENCE SUMMARY.

(Erase heading not required.)

Army Form C. 2118.

Place	Date	Hour	Summary of Events and Information	Remarks and references to Appendices
In the field.	30-7-17	10. P.M.	13th Bn R.W. Fusrs moved up to assembly trenches – Companies taking up their positions as follows:–	13th Bn. R.W. Fusrs. Major
			Reference Map. ST JULIEN. 28. N.W.2. "A" & "B" Coys in HARVEY TRENCH from C.7.d.8½.2 to C.7.c.8½.4½.	
			"C" Coy in ALMA TRENCH and "D" Coy in YORKSHIRE TRENCH.	
			Batt. H.Q. in the deep dugout in YORKSHIRE TRENCH.	
			At 12.30 A.M. (31.7.17) All Companies reported to be in positions.	
			All Bayonets were fixed after positions had been taken up. The Battalion frontage extended from C.7.d.6½.6 to C.7.c.9.8	
			"A" Coy 13th Bn R.W. Fus was allotted the frontage C.7.d.6½.6 to C.8.d.1½.6.	
			"B" " " " " " " C.7.d.4½.6 to C.7.c.9.8.	
			"C" " " " " " " C.8.a.0.2½. to C.7.b.7.5.	
			"D" " " " " " " C.7.b.7.5 to C.7.b.6.7½.	
			Distribution of Officers of the 13th Bn. R.W. Fus going into action were as follows:–	
			BATT. H.Q. Officer Commanding. Lt. Col. R.O. CAMPBELL. D.S.O.	
			Capt. G.H. LEES M.C. (Acting Second-in-Command).	
			Capt & Adjt G.M. JONES	
			Signalling Officer. 2/Lieut J. CYNLAIS EVANS.	

Army Form C. 2118.

Instructions regarding War Diaries and Intelligence Summaries are contained in F. S. Regs., Part II. and the Staff Manual respectively. Title pages will be prepared in manuscript.

WAR DIARY
or
INTELLIGENCE SUMMARY.
(Erase heading not required.)

Place	Date	Hour	Summary of Events and Information	Remarks and references to Appendices
In the Field	30.7.17 (Contd)		"A" Company O.C. Lieut. K. G. EDWARDS. "C" Company. O.C. 2/Lieut. M. M. EVANS. 2/Lieut. T. S. BOWDAGE. "B" Company. O.C. Capt. F. W. VAUGHAN 2/Lieut. G. HOLT. 2/Lieut. WILFRED THOMAS "D" Company O.C. Capt. J. M. OWEN 2/Lieut. C. B. WILLIAMS 2/Lieut W. H. MARTIN Transport Officer 2/Lieut. H. E. R. FORD. 2/Lieut W. Ll. DAVIES	[signature] 13th R.W. Fus Major
			Other Ranks going into action. — 600.	
			31st July 1917. ZERO. DAY.	
" " "	31.7.17	3.50.AM (ZERO)	Our artillery opened a terrific barrage on enemy's front line. Coys 13th Bn. R.W. Fus moved up and took up their positions behind the barrage, ready to advance when the barrage lifted.	
" " "	"	5.20.AM	Message received from O.C. "B" Coy that he had taken the BLUE LINE at 4-50.a.m, and was in touch with 16th Bn. R.W.Fus on his left - his estimated casualties being 6. O.R's. wounded - prisoners coming in large numbers. Captured documents received & forwarded to BRIGADE HEADQUARTERS.	
		5.26am	Message received from O.C. "A" Coy. that he had taken the BLUE LINE at 4.45 a.m and was in touch with troops on his right and left.	
		5.30am.	Message received that BRIGADE HEADQUARTERS had moved to WELSH HARP.	

Instructions regarding War Diaries and Intelligence Summaries are contained in F. S. Regs., Part II. and the Staff Manual respectively. Title Pages will be prepared in manuscript.

WAR DIARY
or
INTELLIGENCE SUMMARY
(Erase heading not required.)

Army Form C. 2118

Place	Date	Hour	Summary of Events and Information	Remarks and references to Appendices
In the field	31.7.17.	6.30 A.M.	Message received from the Signalling Officer that he had established a Forward Command Post in a dugout in the neighbourhood of KIEL COT - 8 prisoners sent by runner and communication established with BRIGADE FORWARD STATION.	[signature] 18th Bn. R.W.F. Major
		6. A.M.	BLACK LINE reported taken.	
		8. A.M.	13th Bn. R.W. Fus established Forward Command Post near TELEGRAPH HOUSE.	
		11. A.M.	BATT. H.Q. established near TELEGRAPH HOUSE.	
		6. P.M.	Forward Command Post moved to large dugout in the BLACK LINE, north of PERISCOPE HOUSE.	
		7. P.M.	BATT H.Q. established in the same place.	
			Capt. J. M. OWEN disabled by gas before reaching objective.	
			2/Lieut: W. H. MARTIN — killed.	
			2/Lieut: W. LL. DAVIES — killed.	
			2/Lieut: M. M. EVANS wounded after taking objective.	
			Estimated Casualties — Other Ranks = 150	

1875 Wt. W593/826 1,000,000 4/15 J.B.C. & A. A.D.S.S./Forms/C. 2118.

Vol 21

13TH BATTN. ROYAL WELSH FUSILIERS

WAR DIARY

AUGUST - 1917

21.B
5 sheets

Army Form C. 2118

Instructions regarding War Diaries and Intelligence Summaries are contained in F. S. Regs., Part II. and the Staff Manual respectively. Title Pages will be prepared in manuscript.

WAR DIARY
or
INTELLIGENCE SUMMARY
(Erase heading not required.)

Place	Date	Hour	Summary of Events and Information	Remarks and references to Appendices
In the field	1-8-17.	......	Ceaseless rain throughout the day and night. Hostile shelling intense at intervals, confined largely to the road between IRON CROSS and Battalion Headquarters. Enemy also put up a heavy barrage on the GREEN LINE and forward of it from about 7-30 P.M. to 8-30 P.M. - At 11-30 P.M. the Battalion moved forward from the BLACK LINE to relieve the 10th Bn. S.W.B. 14th R.W. Fus. and the 17th R.W. Fus. on the STEENBEEK LINE - Relief complete 2-30 A.M. (August 2nd).	A.M. Jones Capt & Adjt 15th R.W.F.
" " "	2-8-17.	......	The ceaseless rain had rendered the ground almost impossible for progress, and "going" was extremely difficult. Enemy's artillery was active but his shooting erratic, and the Battalion suffered no casualties during the relief. The disposition of the Battalion on completion of relief was as follows:- REFERENCE MAP - LANGEMARCK 1/10,000. "B" Coy. held from U.27.d.9.5. to U.27.d.6.7. "A" " " " U.27.d.6.7. to U.27.d.8.9. with the 14th R.W. Fus. on its left. "C" " " " U.27.d.4½.1. to U.27.d.2.5. "D" " " " U.27.d.2.5. to U.27.d.0.9. Batt. Headquarters in concrete dugout at U.27.c.5½.3¼. Throughout the day the enemy shelled our positions heavily, Battalion Headquarters receiving particular attention. Enemy artillery fire became intense about 9-15 P.M. and three separate barrages were put on our positions - one along the STEENBEEK, one in front of BRIERLEY ROAD, and 1 behind BRIERLY ROAD. Movement was also observed in the enemy's positions and O.C. "A" Coy. fired the "S.O.S." rocket. Our artillery opened immediately placing a heavy barrage 100 yards beyond the STEENBEEK.	
" " "	3-8-17.	......	Rain still continued and positions became almost inundated. Enemy artillery not so active as on previous occasions. His shooting was distributed largely on our support lines and increased during the evening. Our artillery kept up a steady fire on enemy's positions throughout the day. "A" Coy. 15th R.W. Fus. relieved the 14th R.W. Fus. their line running from U.27.d.5.6. to U.27.d.8.8. "B" Coy. taking over "A" Coy's portion of the line. There was no change in the support Coys.	
" " "	4-8-17.	......	During the morning, hostile artillery activity was normal. In the afternoon it steadily increased, becoming intense between 3 and 4 P.M. The 15th Bn. R.W. Fus. was relieved by the 10th Bn. Welsh Regt. on the STEENBEEK LINE. On completion of relief Coys. of the 15th R.W. Fus. moved off in the following order to ELVERDINGHE CHATEAU:- C, D, B, A. - relief complete about 12 midnight.	
" " "	5-8-17.	......	The Battalion entrained at ELVERDINGHE at 11 A.M. arriving at PROVEN at [illegible] A.M. From there the Battalion marched to camp at E.H.6.9.4½. (SHEET 27 N.E. BELGIUM & FRANCE).	
" " "	6-8-17.	......	At [illegible] - the [illegible] the day resting.	
" " "	7-8-17.	......	Day spent in cleaning [illegible] & equipment.	

1875 Wt. W593/826 1,000,000 4/15 J.B.C. & A. A.D.S.S./Forms/C. 2118.

Army Form C. 2118

Instructions regarding War Diaries and Intelligence Summaries are contained in F. S. Regs., Part II. and the Staff Manual respectively. Title Pages will be prepared in manuscript.

WAR DIARY
or
INTELLIGENCE SUMMARY
(Erase heading not required.)

Place	Date	Hour	Summary of Events and Information	Remarks and references to Appendices
In the Field	8.8.17	-	Training around billets.	G. M. Jones Capt & Adj. for O.C.
"	9.8.17	-	Training	
"	10.8.17	-	Training	
"	11.8.17	-	Training	
"	12.8.17	-	Brigade Church of England Service in the camp of 16th Bn R.W.F. at 11 a.m.	
"	13.8.17	-	Training	
"	14.8.17	-	Training	
"	15.8.17	-	Training.	
"	16.8.17	-	Training.	
"	17.8.17	-	Training.	
"	18.8.17	-	A. B. & D. Coys left camp in P.5 area - E.16.a.9.4½; Sheet 27 - at 9 a.m. entraining PROVEN at 11 a.m. On arrival at ELVERDINGHE they marched to their respective positions as follows:- A & D Coys.- MACKENSEN FARM (C.8.c.5.7); B Coy to shelters near AUSTERLITZ FARM (B.30.a.0.7) [Map: ST. JULIEN - 28. N.W] Major Bell took command of the 3 Coys. acting under the instructions of A.A. & Q.M.G, 38th (Welsh) Division. Transport moved off from P.5 AREA at 1.30 p.m. under Brigade Transport Officer to BRIDGE JUNCTION. The remainder of the Battalion left camp in P.5 AREA at 2.15 p.m. entraining at PROVEN at 4 p.m. On arrival at ELVERDINGHE they marched to shelters in the MALAKOFF FARM AREA (B.22.d)	
"	19.8.17	-	The 13th R.W.F. with the exception of A. B & D. Coys. moved from camp in B.22.d to camp in B.23.a. Work on new range at B.23.b.8.7½.	
"	20.8.17	-	"C" Coy. did a tactical scheme in the morning and relieved "A" Coy. at MACKENSEN FARM in the afternoon. New Brigade Rifle Range at B.23.b.8.7½ completed.	
"	21.8.17	-	"A" Coy. did a tactical scheme in the morning, and firing on the range during the afternoon. Rifle Grenade Demonstration at FRIEDLAND FARM at 11 a.m; Lewis Gunners on Range.	

875 Wt. W593/826 1,000,000 4/15 J.B.C. & A. A.D.S.S./Forms/C. 2118.

Army Form C. 2118

Instructions regarding War Diaries and Intelligence Summaries are contained in F. S. Regs., Part II. and the Staff Manual respectively. Title Pages will be prepared in manuscript.

WAR DIARY
or
INTELLIGENCE SUMMARY
(Erase heading not required.)

Place	Date	Hour	Summary of Events and Information	Remarks and references to Appendices
In the Field	22.8.17	-	"A" Coy. training during the morning. Relief of "D" Coy. by "A" Coy. at MACKENSEN FARM in the afternoon. Lewis Gunners on Range. Lt. Colonel R.O. Campbell, D.S.O. proceeded on leave, and Major F. S. Lloyd took command of the Battalion.	[illegible signature]
"	23.8.17	-	Training – At 3 pm. the 13th R.W.F. with the exception of A. B & C. Coys moved from Camp in B 23.a to shelters near HULL'S FARM – move completed 4 pm.	
"	24.8.17	-	A. B & C. Coys. left their respective positions at 8 a.m. rejoining the Battalion near HULL'S FARM. The 13th R.W.F. relieved the 14th R.W.F. and became the leading battalion of the Support Brigade in CANDLE TRENCH on the PILCKEM RIDGE – Relief commenced at 1.45 pm. and was completed at 4 pm.	
"	25.8.17	-	Working Parties supplied in accordance with Brigade Working Party Table.	
"	26.8.17	-	" " " " " " " " " "	
"	27.8.17	-	" " " " " " " " " "	
"	28.8.17	-	" " " " " " " " " "	
"	29.8.17	-	The 113th Bde relieved the 115th Bde in the Divisional Front; the 13th R.W.F. relieving the 10th Bn. S.W.B. in support. Relief commenced 12 midnight and completed 1 a.m. (30th) Coys. of the 13th R.W. Fus. moved from CANDLE TRENCH in the following order:- A. Coy. 11.5 pm; B. Coy. 11.15 pm; C. Coy. 11.25 pm. D Coy. 11.35 pm; Battn H.Q. 11.45 pm; The relief was not interfered with by hostile shelling although enemy shelled intermittently, but shooting was erratic. On completion of relief the following dispositions were taken up by Coys:- "A" Coy. from U.28.d.55.35 to U.28.d.45.45 – Coy. H.Qrs. U.28.d.45.40; B. Coy. from U.28.d.2½.8 to U.28.d.3.8¾ – Coy H.Qrs AU BON GITE; "C" Coy. from U.28.d.45.45 to U.28.d.40.50 – Coy H.Q. U.28.d.45.40; "D" Coy:- RÊITRES FARM U.22.c.9.1½ to U.22.d.1½. Coy. H.Qrs. RÊITRES FARM; BATTN. H.QRS – AU BON GITE.	
"	30.8.17	-	Situation normal – Intermittent hostile shelling throughout the day confined largely around Battn. Headquarters and the STEENBEEK VALLEY.	

1875 Wt. W593/826 1,000,000 4/15 J.B.C. & A. A.D.S.S./Forms/C. 2118.

Army Form C. 2118

Instructions regarding War Diaries and Intelligence Summaries are contained in F. S. Regs., Part II. and the Staff Manual respectively. Title Pages will be prepared in manuscript.

WAR DIARY
or
INTELLIGENCE SUMMARY
(Erase heading not required.)

Place	Date	Hour	Summary of Events and Information	Remarks and references to Appendices
In the Field	31.8.17	–	Hostile artillery active. Back areas shelled intermittently throughout the day.	G. Jones Capt. Adjt. for Lt Col.

1875 Wt. W593/826 1,000,000 4/15 J.B.C. & A. A.D.S.S./Forms/C. 2118.

13th Batt Royal Welsh Fusiliers

Vol 22

War Diary

for

September 1917.

22 B.
Sept

Army Form C. 2118

Instructions regarding War Diaries and Intelligence Summaries are contained in F. S. Regs., Part II. and the Staff Manual respectively. Title Pages will be prepared in manuscript.

WAR DIARY
or
INTELLIGENCE SUMMARY
(Erase heading not required.)

Place	Date	Hour	Summary of Events and Information	Remarks and references to Appendices
In the field.	1-9-17.	....	The 13th Bn. R.W.Fus. relieved the 16th Bn. R.W.Fusrs. in the Right Front. Relief commenced at 9P.M. and was complete by 11.30 P.M. The disposition of Coys. on completion of relief were as follows:- Reference Map – BROMBEEK. 1/10,000. A Coy. 13 R.W.Fus. [RIGHT FRONT] holding a line from U.30.a. 40. 95. to U.24.c. 00.55. 'B' " " " [RIGHT SUPPORT]. U29 d 5.6. to U.29.b. 0.1. 'C' " " " [LEFT FRONT]. holding a line from U 24.c. 00.35 to U.23.d.55.65. 'D' " " " in Reserve occupying concrete dug-outs at U.29.a.45.90. BATTALION HEADQUARTERS in concrete dug-out near ALOUETTE FARM. (U.29.a.90.40.). Hostile shelling during relief was slight and no casualties were suffered.	R O Campbell Lt:Col: Commanding 13th Bn. R.W. Fusiliers.
" " "	2-9-17.	....	Between the period 1 – 4 A.M. enemy shelled our support lines heavily, BATT. H.Q. receiving particular attention. At dawn hostile aeroplanes were extremely active flying low over our lines and firing upon our positions. During the whole day visibility was excellent and artillery on both sides active. Our front line was not subjected to any heavy hostile shelling, and enemy's shooting was distributed mainly on our support lines, BATT. H.Q. and the STEENBEEK VALLEY. At 9 P.M. he opened a standing barrage on the road from ALOUETTE FARM to LANGEMARCK, lasting until 11 P.M. – this fire was more or less continuous until dawn when it slackened considerably. MAJOR O.J. BELL, 2nd in command, slightly wounded, and Medical Officer.	
" " "	3-9-17.		Hostile artillery activity was again considerable and visibility good. Aerial activity on both sides was above normal and several engagements took place. Between 9 and 11 P.M. hostile shelling reached its greatest intensity, after which it slackened. Our artillery successfully engaged enemy batteries and targets behind his lines during the day.	
" " "	4-9-17.		Between 2 and 4 A.M. enemy shelling was intense but shooting erratic. MAJOR F.S. LLOYD, Commanding 13th Bn. R.W.Fus. severely wounded, and 2nd LIEUT. J. PRITCHARD killed. – CAPT. R.M. WYNN EDWARDS took over command of the Battalion. Hostile artillery kept up a steady fire during the whole day. His shooting was confined to the usual targets in our support lines. Our own artillery was extremely active and successfully engaged enemy batteries and targets behind his lines. At 5 P.M. 38th Divisional Artillery put a practice barrage on enemy's front line lasting until 5-10 P.M. – Enemy's retaliation was slight. – The night was quieter than usual.	

1875 Wt. W593/826 1,000,000 4/15 J.B.C. & A. A.D.S.S./Forms/C. 2118.

Instructions regarding War Diaries and Intelligence Summaries are contained in F. S. Regs., Part II. and the Staff Manual respectively. Title Pages will be prepared in manuscript.

WAR DIARY
or
INTELLIGENCE SUMMARY
(Erase heading not required.)

Army Form C. 2118

Place	Date	Hour	Summary of Events and Information	Remarks and references to Appendices
In the field	4-9-17.	(continued)	The 13th Bn. R.W. Fus. relieved by the 10th Bn. Welch Regiment in the RIGHT FRONT. Relief commenced at 9 P.M. and was complete by 11-30 P.M. Hostile artillery was quieter than usual, and the relief was not interfered with. - On completion of relief the 13th Bn. R.W. Fus. moved to camp at B.22.d.7.7. - Reference Map ST JULIEN. 28.N.W.	R D Campbell Lt Col. Commanding 13th Bn R.W. Fusiliers.
" " "	5-9-17.	......	The day was spent in overhauling and cleaning kits & equipment.	
" " "	6-9-17	......	Company Training.	
" " "	7-9-17	......	Training.	
" " "	8-9-17	......	Training.	
" " "	9-9-17	......	Church services in camp.	
" " "	10-9-17	......	The 13th Bn. R.W. Fus. relieved by the 6th Bn. K.S.L.I. in camp at B.22.d.7.7. - On relief the 13th R.W. Fus. marched to ELVERDINGHE where the Battalion entrained for INTERNATIONAL CORNER STATION. - From there the Battalion marched to ~~camp~~ at SUTTON CAMP (near PROVEN).	
" " "	11-9-17	...	Training and baths.	
" " "	12-9-17	...	Training.	
" " "	13-9-17	......	Training.	
" " "	14-9-17	......	The 113th Infantry Brigade commenced to move to the XI Corps area by march route. - The 13th Bn. R.W. Fus. left SUTTON CAMP at 11 A.M. and marched to the EECQU AREA (Q.7.a.0.6). - The 13th R.W. Fus. billetted for the night, arriving in billets about 4-30 P.M.	
" " "	15-9-17	......	The 13th Bn. R.W. Fus. moved off from the EECQU AREA at 9 A.M. and marched to the MORBECQUE AREA, arriving in billets about 4 P.M. The Batt. billetted for the night in MORBECQUE. - MARCH ROUTE - VIA ST SYLVESTRE [?] CAPPELLE & HAZEBROUCK.	
" " "	16-9-17	......	The 13th Bn. R.W. Fus. moved off from MORBECQUE at 10 A.M. and marched to the ESTAIRES AREA, arriving in billets about 4-30 P.M. The Batt. billetted for the night in ESTAIRES. - MARCH ROUTE taken VIA MERVILLE.	
" " "	17-9-17	......	The 13th Bn. R.W. Fus. moved off from ESTAIRES at 11 A.M. and marched to ERQUINGHEM VIA BAC-ST-MAUR, relieving the 2nd/10th Bn. King's Liverpool Regiment in Brigade Reserve. - Relief at ERQUINGHEM complete at 1-30 P.M. 'A' Coy. 13th R.W. Fus. relieved 'A' Coy. 2/10th Bn. K.L.R. in support in the SUBSIDIARY LINE. Relief commenced 8 P.M. and completed by 9-30 P.M. Coy. H.Q. at I.20.a.60.75.	

1875 Wt. W593/826 1,000,000 4/15 J.B.C. & A. A.D.S.S./Forms/C. 2118.

Army Form C. 2118

Instructions regarding War Diaries and Intelligence Summaries are contained in F. S. Regs., Part II. and the Staff Manual respectively. Title Pages will be prepared in manuscript.

WAR DIARY
or
INTELLIGENCE SUMMARY
(Erase heading not required.)

Place	Date	Hour	Summary of Events and Information	Remarks and references to Appendices
[illegible] In the field	18-9-17	....	Training	R.D. Campbell Lt:Col: Commanding 13th R.W. Fusiliers.
" " "	19-9-17	.....	Training. - 'B' Coy, 13th R.W.Fus. relieved 'A' Coy 13th RWFus. in support in the SUBSIDIARY LINE. - Relief commenced 8 P.M. and was complete by 9-30 P.M.	
" " "	20-9-17	......	Training.	
" " "	21-9-17.	....	Training. - 'C' Coy. 13th R.W.Fus. relieved 'B' Coy. 13th R.W.Fus. in Support in the SUBSIDIARY LINE. - Relief complete - 9-45 P.M.	
" " "	22-9-17.	.....	Training.	
" " "	23-9-17	.....	13th Bn. R.W.Fus. relieved 16th Bn. R.W.Fus in the RUE DE BOIS SUBSECTION of the BOIS GRENIER SECTION. Relief complete about 11 P.M. - Dispositions on completion of relief were as follows: Map Reference:- BOIS GRENIER Sheet: 36.N.W.4. 'A' Coy. 13th R.W.Fus. - RIGHT FRONT. COY. H.Q. I.21. a. ½. 4¾. 'B' Coy " " - CENTRE FRONT. COY. H.Q. I.15.c. 70. 45. 'C' Coy " " - LEFT FRONT COY. HQ. I.9.d. 50. 14. 'D' Coy " " - SUPPORT [SUBSIDIARY LINE]. Coy H.Q. I.14. b. 75. 10. BATT. H.Q. " " " - SUBSIDIARY LINE. I.14.d. 5¼. 8¼. Battalion front extended roughly from BURNT FARM (I.20.d.) to PEAR TREE Fm. (I.16.b.).	
" " " "	24-9-17.	......	artillery on both sides quiet. - Enemy artillery fired during the day as follows. - 7-30. A.M. - two 77 mm shells on front line about I.21.a. 9.9. also a few on WELLINGTON AVENUE. Vicinity of DESOLANQUE Fm also received slight attention. 8-30 P.M. enemy sent over about 10 L.T.M.'s on STURT TRENCH. possibly in retaliation for our M.T.M.'s fired at 1 P.M. The night was quiet with the exception of machine gun activity on both sides.	
" " "	25-9-17	.....	A quiet day. Hostile artillery fired 3 salvoes of 77 mm. shells on COWGATE AVENUE at 4-15 P.M. also a few shells into ARMENTIERES at 2-15 P.M. L.T.M.'s also fired by enemy on PEAR TREE. Our activity fired on targets in enemy's lines and our heavies periodically into WEZ MACQUART. - Night quiet. Aerial activity on both sides normal.	
[illegible]	[illegible]	.....	A patrol left our lines at 5-5 A.M. to deal with enemy working party in INCOME TRENCH (I.21.d.). - 16 Rifle grenades fired and party dispersed. 'D' Coy. [illegible] (support Coy) relieved 'C' Coy 13 R.W.F. in the Left Front.	
" " "	26-9-17.	.....	Hostile artillery more active than on previous days owing to improved visibility. Points fired upon as follows:- 10-15 - 11-30 A.M. sundry rounds fired in the vicinity of DESOLANQUE Fm. (I.14.d.). 9-P.M. - a few salvoes fired into CHAPPELLE D'ARMENTIERES. 9-11 P.M. Occasional shells fired but on no fixed targets.. Our artillery fired occasional bursts during the day on enemy's lines. - Heavies on targets in WEZ MACQUART.	
" " "	27-9-17	.....	A very quiet day. - Artillery activity on both sides below normal apparently owing to poor visibility. 6 A.M. our artillery fired several bursts of shrapnel on suspected hostile working party in INCOME TRENCH (I.21.d.). Enemy retaliated slightly. 'C' Coy. 13th RW Fus. (support Coy) relieved 'B' Coy in Centre Front - relief complete 11 P.M.	

1875 Wt. W593/826 1,000,000 4/15 J.B.C. & A. A.D.S.S./Forms/C. 2118.

Army Form C. 2118

Instructions regarding War Diaries and Intelligence Summaries are contained in F. S. Regs., Part II. and the Staff Manual respectively. Title Pages will be prepared in manuscript.

WAR DIARY
or
INTELLIGENCE SUMMARY
(Erase heading not required.)

Place	Date	Hour	Summary of Events and Information	Remarks and references to Appendices
In the field.	28-9-17.		Hostile artillery quiet the whole day. A few salvoes of 77 mm shells fired into CHAPELLE D'ARMENTIERES at 7 P.M. — Our artillery engaged various targets on enemy's lines during the day. — Visibility during the day was fair, improving towards evening. Aerial activity on both sides normal.	[illegible] Lt. Col. Commanding 13th R.W. Fusiliers
"	29-9-17.		Our heavy artillery active on hostile batteries between 3 & 6 P.M. also firing into WEZ MACQUART. — The 13th Bn. R.W. Fus. relieved the 14th Bn. R.W. Fus. in the RUE DE BOIS SUBSECTION of the BOIS GRENIER SECTION. — Relief completed about 11 P.M. On completion of relief Companies took up the following dispositions — A & C Coys. billeted in ERQUINGHEM. also BATT. H.Q. B & D Coys. in support in SUBSIDIARY LINE.	
"	30-9-17.		Hostile aerial activity considerable on right area from 2 to 5 P.M. One of our aeroplanes attacked by 4 hostile planes over ERQUINGHEM with no result. — 8 P.M. hostile H.V. GUN firing shrapnel into ARMENTIERES.	

1875 Wt. W593/826 1,000,000 4/15 J.B.C. & A. A.D.S.S./Forms/C. 2118.

13th BATT. ROYAL WELSH FUSILIERS.

Vol 23

WAR DIARY

FOR

OCTOBER 1917.

23 B.
5 sheets

Instructions regarding War Diaries and Intelligence Summaries are contained in F. S. Regs., Part II. and the Staff Manual respectively. Title pages will be prepared in manuscript.

WAR DIARY
or
INTELLIGENCE SUMMARY.
(Erase heading not required.)

Army Form C. 2118.

Place	Date	Hour	Summary of Events and Information	Remarks and references to Appendices

2351 Wt W.... D. D. & L. A.D.S.S. Forms/C 2118

Instructions regarding War Diaries and Intelligence Summaries are contained in F. S. Regs., Part II. and the Staff Manual respectively. Title pages will be prepared in manuscript.

WAR DIARY
or
INTELLIGENCE SUMMARY.
(Erase heading not required.)

October

Army Form C. 2118.

Place	Date	Hour	Summary of Events and Information	Remarks and references to Appendices
In the field	(cont) 9/10/17	–	During this tour in the line the battalion has done a great amount of patrol work, and much valuable information has been obtained.	
"	10/10/17	–	One platoon of the 17th Bn No 5 Port. Bde C.E.P. attached to each of our companies for instruction	
"	11/10/17	–	13th R.W.F. relieved by 16th R.W.F. in the BOIS GRENIER SECTOR (LEFT SUBSECT.) "A" Coy of the 13th Bn remaining behind in the SUBSIDIARY LINE as [illegible] Coy. Each of the Portuguese platoons remained in the line with the 16th Bn	
"	12/10/17	–	Training under arrangements of O.C. Bn and in accordance with Programme of Work submitted by him.	
"	13/10/17	–	Training in accordance with Programme of Training submitted by the Commanding Officer.	
"	14/10/17	–	Church Parades only. At 5-30 pm. "C" Coy moved off from billets to relieve 'A' Coy in the SUBSIDIARY LINE (Right sector). Relief Complete 10.50 pm.	
"	15/10/17	–	Lt Col. Campbell D.S.O. assumed Temporary command of the 113 Inf. Bde in the absence of Brig. Gen. Pryce Davies. In the meantime Capt. R.M. Wynne-Edwards M.C. assumed Command of the 13th Bn R.W.F.	

G.H. Lees Major
13th R.W.F.

2353 Wt. W2544/1454 700,000 5/15 D. D. & L. A.D.S.S./Forms/C. 2118.

Army Form C. 2118.

Instructions regarding War Diaries and Intelligence Summaries are contained in F. S. Regs., Part II, and the Staff Manual respectively. Title pages will be prepared in manuscript.

WAR DIARY
or
INTELLIGENCE SUMMARY.
(Erase heading not required.)

Place	Date	Hour	Summary of Events and Information	Remarks and references to Appendices

D. D. & L. A.D.S.S. Forms/C. 2118

Instructions regarding War Diaries and Intelligence Summaries are contained in F. S. Regs., Part II. and the Staff Manual respectively. Title pages will be prepared in manuscript.

WAR DIARY
or
INTELLIGENCE SUMMARY.
(Erase heading not required.)

October

Army Form C. 2118.

Place	Date	Hour	Summary of Events and Information	Remarks and references to Appendices
In Refuly	23/10/17	–	13th Bn R.W.F. relieved by the 16th R.W.F. Battalion all in billets 9-30 p.m.	
" " "	24/10/17	–	Training in accordance with programme of training arranged by Commanding Officer	
" " "	25/10/17	–	Training in accordance with Programme of Training	
" " "	26/10/17	–	" " " " " " " Lt Col. Campbell D.S.O. proceeded on special leave to England.	
" " "	27/10/17	–	Training in accordance with Programme of Training	
" " "	28/10/17	–	" " " " " " "	
" " "	29/10/17	–	" " " " " " " . In the evening the 13th Bn R.W.F. relieved the 16th R.W.F. in the left Subsection of the BOIS GRENIER sector. The battalion left billets at 5-30 p.m. and relief was completed at 8-15 p.m.	
" " "	30/10/17	–	Desultory artillery & trench mortar fire by both sides throughout the morning.	
" " "	31/10/17		Nothing of importance to report. Situation normal.	G H Lees. Major 13 RWF

2353 Wt. W2544/1454 700,000 5/15 D. D. & L. A.D.S.S./Forms/C. 2118.

Vol 24

13th BATT. ROYAL WELSH FUSILIERS

WAR DIARY

FOR

NOVEMBER 1917

Army Form C. 2118.

WAR DIARY
or
INTELLIGENCE SUMMARY.
(Erase heading not required.)

November

Instructions regarding War Diaries and Intelligence Summaries are contained in F. S. Regs., Part II. and the Staff Manual respectively. Title pages will be prepared in manuscript.

Place	Date	Hour	Summary of Events and Information	Remarks and references to Appendices
In the field	1/11/17		Intermittent shelling and trench mortar fire by both sides during morning and afternoon.	J. F. Leman Lt Col. Comdg 13th RWF
" " "	2/11/17		Situation quiet. Artillery & trench mortars on both sides fairly active throughout the afternoon. Enemy machine gun fire above the normal during the night.	
" " "	3/11/17		The 10th Battn C.E.P. (Portuguese) took over the section of front from PARK ROW AVENUE to WINE AVENUE exclusive, but inclusive of C H Q at the ORCHARD, 2 Coys relieving A. Coy 13th RWF in the front line with the exception of CISSIE POST; 2 Coys relieving B. Coy 16th RWF in the centre and right of Subsidiary Line. Relief complete 8.50 PM. On completion of relief A Coy 13th RWF moved to Left Subsidiary line relieving C Coy 16th RWF. Relief complete 10.0 PM.	
	4/11/17		Two companies of 16th RWF relieved 2 coys of 13th RWF on the LEFT front & subsidiary lines of the BOIS GRENIER SECTOR (LEFT SUBSECTION)	
	5/11/17		Parades for baths and training under company arrangements. Major J. F. Leman assumed command of the Battalion vice Major G. H. Lees M.C.	
	6/11/17		Training in accordance with programme of training submitted by the Commanding Officer	
	7/11/17		" " " " " " " " "	

2353 Wt. W2544/1454 700,000 5/15 D. D. & L. A.D.S.S./Forms/C 2118.

Instructions regarding War Diaries and Intelligence Summaries are contained in F. S. Regs., Part II. and the Staff Manual respectively. Title pages will be prepared in manuscript.

WAR DIARY
or
INTELLIGENCE SUMMARY.
(Erase heading not required.)

November

Army Form C. 2118.

Place	Date	Hour	Summary of Events and Information	Remarks and references to Appendices
	[illegible]		[illegible] ... at I [illegible] with the object of killing [illegible] ... At Zero hour (12 am) [illegible] ...	
			[illegible]	
			R.W. Kent relieved [illegible] in the left sub-sector of the BOIS [illegible] sector.	
			[illegible] after relief were as follows: Left front C Coy. Centre front B Coy. Right front D Coy.	
			Relief complete [illegible]	
	[illegible]		Situation normal. In the afternoon Trench Mortars on both sides fairly active.	
	[illegible]		[illegible] Nothing of importance to report	
	[illegible]		[illegible] relieved C Coy on the left front sector. Relief complete 6.35 pm.	
			At [illegible] enemy put over heavy barrage of gas shells, trench mortars & 77mm on Right front sector [illegible]	

2355 Wt W3[illegible] D. D. & L. A.D.S.S./Forms/C. 2118.

Instructions regarding War Diaries and Intelligence Summaries are contained in F. S. Regs., Part II. and the Staff Manual respectively. Title pages will be prepared in manuscript.

WAR DIARY
or
INTELLIGENCE SUMMARY. November

(*Erase heading not required.*)

Army Form C. 2118.

Place	Date	Hour	Summary of Events and Information	Remarks and references to Appendices
In the field	14/11/17		Situation normal. A fighting Patrol of 2 officers (2nd Lt. W. Roberts + 2nd Lt J.C. Palmer) 2 Sgts + 19 O.R. went out from CISSIE POST with the object of entering Gap in enemy wire at I 22 a 20.50 and securing indentifications. A party of enemy were encountered lying in wait in Gap, who opened fire at close range with an Automatic rifle, causing some casualties. Our patrol replied with rapid fire. Enemy losses believed to be heavy. All our casualties were brought back to our line, a distance of 500 yds. They were, killed 1 Sergt + 1 O.R. Wounded 1 officer (2nd Lt J.C. Palmer) and 5. O.R. As a result of this enterprise, the following were recommended by the C.O., 2nd Lt W. Roberts, Pte E. Cornish, Sgt E.A. Jones, and Corporal A.J. Williams.	J.G. Dennis Lt Col comdg 13th RWF
"	15/11/17		Situation quiet. Between 3 to 3.30 AM Enemy sent gas shells on LEFT COY SECTOR	
"	16.11.17		In the BOIS GRENIER SECTOR, LEFT SUB-SECTION. 16th RWF relieved 13th RWF. B + D Coys of 13th RWF going out to billets at ERQUINGHEM. A + C Coys occupying LEFT + RIGHT SECTORS of SUBSIDUARY LINE. RELIEF complete at 8.0 pm	
"	17.11.17		B + D Coys of 13th R.W.F. Inspections + Bathing Parades (at BAC ST MAUR)	
"	18.11.17		B + D Coys of 13th R.W.F. CHURCH Parades.	
"	19.11.17		Training under Company arrangements at ERQUINGHEM. Inter-company relief. A + C Coys 13th RWF relieved by B + D Coys 13th R.W.F. RELIEF COMPLETE AT 9.0 pm	

2353 Wt. W2544/1454 700,000 5/15 D. D. & L. A.D.S.S. Forms/C. 2118.

Army Form C. 2118.

Instructions regarding War Diaries and Intelligence Summaries are contained in F. S. Regs., Part II and the Staff Manual respectively. Title pages will be prepared in manuscript.

WAR DIARY
or
INTELLIGENCE SUMMARY.
(Erase heading not required.)

Place	Date	Hour	Summary of Events and Information	Remarks and references to Appendices

2337 Wt W..... D. D. & L. A.D.S.S./Forms/C. 2118.

Instructions regarding War Diaries and Intelligence Summaries are contained in F. S. Regs., Part II. and the Staff Manual respectively. Title pages will be prepared in manuscript.

WAR DIARY
or
INTELLIGENCE SUMMARY.
(Erase heading not required.)

NOVEMBER

Army Form C. 2118.

Place	Date	Hour	Summary of Events and Information	Remarks and references to Appendices
In the field	25/11/17		Visibility good. high wind. During forenoon to 2 pm our Artillery fired about 250 rounds (18 pdrs) vicinity of GODDARDS HOUSE Very little retaliation nothing unusual, quiet day! Inter-Company relief "B" Coy 13th RWF relieved "A" Coy 13th RWF on LEFT Coy FRONT. "D" Coy 13th RWF relieved "C" Coy 13th R.W.F. on CENTRE Coy FRONT. Relief complete @ 6.0 pm. Dispositions after relief:- "A" Coy ~~R~~ LEFT SUB. LINE, "B" Coy LEFT FRONT LINE; "C" Coy CENTRE SUB LINE; "D" Coy CENTRE FRONT LINE.	
" "	26/11/17		Situation quiet. Rather more Artillery activity. Fair visibility.	
" "	27/11/17		Situation quiet. Artillery fire below normal - poor visibility. Increased machine gun activity at night.	
" "	28/11/17		Concentrated shoot on INCLINE SUPPORT TRENCH by our heavies + trench mortars 1 to 3 p.m. Vigorous retaliation by enemy during same hours - several direct hits on Signal Box at I 14 b 50.10. The 13th RWF relieved by 16th RWF in BOIS GRENIER SECTOR (LEFT SUBSECTION) left and centre positions. Relief complete 8.5 pm. All in billets 9.50 pm.	
" "	29/11/17		A, B & D Coys of 13th RWF relieved 1 Coy of 16th RWF, 1 Coy 14th RWF + 2 Coys 17th CEP	

J F [illegible] Cmdg 13th RWF

2353 Wt. W2544/1454 700,000 5/15 D. D. & L. A.D.S.S. Forms/C. 2118.

Instructions regarding War Diaries and Intelligence Summaries are contained in F. S. Regs., Part II. and the Staff Manual respectively. Title pages will be prepared in manuscript.

WAR DIARY
or
INTELLIGENCE SUMMARY.
(Erase heading not required.)

NOVEMBER

Army Form C. 2118.

Place	Date	Hour	Summary of Events and Information	Remarks and references to Appendices
[illegible]	[illegible]		in the [illegible] CRATER Salisbury line. Relief complete 7.30 pm	
			C Coy [illegible] at [illegible]	
[illegible]	[illegible]		C Coy [illegible] relieved A Coy [illegible] in the Salisbury line [illegible]	
			A Coy [illegible] at [illegible] [illegible] complete 6.0 pm	

[illegible] Lt Col

2355 Wt W2544/1454 700,000 4/15 D. D. & L. A.D.S.S./Forms/C. 2118.

13th. BATT. ROYAL WELSH FUSILIERS

Vol 25

WAR DIARY

FOR

DECEMBER 1917

25B
5 sheets

Instructions regarding War Diaries and Intelligence Summaries are contained in F. S. Regs., Part II. and the Staff Manual respectively. Title pages will be prepared in manuscript.

WAR DIARY
or
INTELLIGENCE SUMMARY.
(Erase heading not required.)

Army Form C. 2118.

DECEMBER 1915

Place	Date	Hour	Summary of Events and Information	Remarks and references to Appendices
[illegible]	1st		A Coy 13th RIF relieved D Coy 13th RIF in Subsidiary Line, BOIS GRENIER SECTOR. D Coy occupying billets at QUATRE CHEMINS. Relief complete 6 p.m.	
[illegible]	2nd		D Coy 13th RIF relieved B Coy 13th RIF in Subsidiary Line BOIS GRENIER SECTOR. B Coy occupying billets at QUATRE CHEMINS. Relief complete 6 p.m.	
[illegible]	3rd		13th RIF relieved 16th RIR in front line of BOIS GRENIER SECTOR. Relief complete 6.20 p.m. Dispositions after relief are as follows:- D Coy in Front, A Coy Centre Front, C Coy Reinforcement, B Coy in Subsidiary Line.	

W. W. [illegible] D. D. & L. A.D.S.S. Forms/C. 2118

Instructions regarding War Diaries and Intelligence Summaries are contained in F. S. Regs., Part II. and the Staff Manual respectively. Title pages will be prepared in manuscript.

WAR DIARY
or
INTELLIGENCE SUMMARY.
(Erase heading not required.)

DECEMBER 1917.

Army Form C. 2118.

Place	Date	Hour	Summary of Events and Information	Remarks and references to Appendices
In the field	7/12/17		Visibility poor. Enemy TMs very active during forenoon. Number of our aircraft up observing. Our artillery fires in retaliation. The 16th RWF relieved	
" " "	[illegible]		the 13th RWF in the LEFT SUBSECTION of BOIS GRENIER SECTOR. Relief complete 6.40.	
			the 13th RWF proceeded to billets at ERQUINGHAM & LA ROLANDERIE	
" " "	8/12/17		Companies paraded for baths	
" " "	9/12/17		Church parades only	
" " "	10/12/17		Training under company arrangements.	
" " "	11/12/17		The 13th RWF relieved 16th RWF in LEFT SUB SECTION of BOIS GRENIER SECTOR	
			Relief complete 6.35 pm.	
" " "	12/12/17		Considerable aerial activity. Machine guns fairly active during night.	
			1 enemy plane crashed in flames over ARMENTIERES.	
" " "	13/12/17		Quiet day, nothing to report	
" " "	14/12/17		Enemy TMs & artillery rather more active. Movement reported behind enemy lines	
" " "	15/12/17		The 16th RWF relieved the 13th RWF in the LEFT SUBSECTION of BOIS GRENIER SECTOR	
			and the 13th RWF relieved the 14th RWF in the SUBSIDIARY LINE.	
" " "	16/12/17		In the Subsidiary line. Working parties. A Coy went back to billets at QUATRE CHEMINS	G H Lee Major Comdg 13th RW Fusiliers

2353 Wt. W2544/1454 700,000 5/15 D. D. & L. A.D.S.S./Forms/C. 2118.

Army Form C. 2118.

WAR DIARY
or
INTELLIGENCE SUMMARY.
(Erase heading not required.)

Instructions regarding War Diaries and Intelligence Summaries are contained in F. S. Regs., Part II. and the Staff Manual respectively. Title pages will be prepared in manuscript.

Place	Date	Hour	Summary of Events and Information	Remarks and references to Appendices

Instructions regarding War Diaries and Intelligence Summaries are contained in F. S. Regs., Part II. and the Staff Manual respectively. Title pages will be prepared in manuscript.

WAR DIARY
or
INTELLIGENCE SUMMARY.
(*Erase heading not required.*)

DECEMBER

Army Form C. 2118.

Place	Date	Hour	Summary of Events and Information	Remarks and references to Appendices
In the field	24/12/17 (contd)		Two patrols sent out after raiders had been driven off failed to get any identifications. The 16th RWF relieved the 13th RWF in the LEFT SUBSECTION of FLEURBAIX SECTOR. The 13th RWF going out to billets in FLEURBAIX. All in billets 8. pm.	Major Comdg 13th RWFusiliers
" " "	25/12/17		Church parade in the morning. Dinners to C & D Coys in the afternoon.	
" " "	26/12/17		Bathing parades morning and afternoon. Dinners to A & B Coys in the afternoon.	
" " "	27/12/17		250 men on a working party engaged in burying cable.	
	28/12/17		The 13th RWF relieved the 15th RWF in the RIGHT SUBSECTION of the BOIS GRENIER SECTOR. Relief complete 7.15. Dispositions after relief were as follows. C Coy right front; D Coy left front; B Coy left support; A Coy right support. Relief complete 7.15 pm	
	29/12/17		Situation normal, nothing special to report	
	30/12/17		" " . Trench mortars rather more active.	
	31/12/17		Quiet day. Some aeroplane activity during the afternoon.	[illegible signature]

2353 Wt. W2544/1454 700,000 5/15 D. D. & L. A.D.S.S./Forms/C. 2118.

1st Batt ROYAL WELSH FUSILIERS

Vol 26

WAR DIARY

FOR

JANUARY 1918

Instructions regarding War Diaries and Intelligence Summaries are contained in F. S. Regs., Part II. and the Staff Manual respectively. Title Pages will be prepared in manuscript.

WAR DIARY
or
INTELLIGENCE SUMMARY
(Erase heading not required.)

January 1918

Army Form C. 2118

Place	Date	Hour	Summary of Events and Information	Remarks and references to Appendices
In the field	1/1/18		{Capt. G. M. Jones (Adjt) & Lieuts. H. E. R. Ford & S. Hull awarded the MILITARY CROSS {Trench mortars on both sides fairly active. Increased activity in the air.	J F Leman Lt Col
	2/1/18		Normal situation. Enemy machine guns very active during the night.	
	3/1/18		Artillery on both sides active above normal throughout the day.	
	4/1/18		Situation normal, nothing to report.	
	5/1/18		The 15th R.I.F. relieved the 13th R.I.F. in the CENTRE SECTION BOIS GRENIER. Relief complete 8.55 pm. The 13th R.I.F. relieved the 16th R.I.F. in the RIGHT SUBSECTION FLEURBAIX. Relief complete 9.55 p.m. A considerable amount of [illegible] in front of SUBSIDIARY and SUPPORT LINES was done by the battalion during this tour in the line.	
	6/1/18		Enemy Trench mortars very active during the afternoon. Situation normal.	
"	7/1/18		Trench mortars on both sides active during the afternoon.	
"	8/1/18		Situation normal, nothing to report.	
"	9/1/18		The 11th R.I.F. relieved the 13th R.I.F. in RIGHT SUBSECTION, FLEURBAIX. Relief complete 6.5 pm. All in billets 8.10 p.m. [FLEURBAIX AREA]	
"	10/1/18		Bathing parades morning and afternoon	
"	11/1/18		Lt Col J. F. LEMAN returned from leave & resumed command of the battalion vice Maj. G. H. [illegible]. Bathing parades and training under company arrangements.	
"	12/1/18		Kit inspections and training under company arrangements during morning.	

1875 Wt. W593/826 1,000,000 4/15 J.B.C. & A. A.D.S.S./Forms/C. 2118.

Army Form C. 2118

Instructions regarding War Diaries and Intelligence Summaries are contained in F. S. Regs., Part II. and the Staff Manual respectively. Title Pages will be prepared in manuscript.

WAR DIARY
or
INTELLIGENCE SUMMARY
(Erase heading not required.)

Place	Date	Hour	Summary of Events and Information	Remarks and references to Appendices
			[illegible]	

1875 Wt. W593/826 1,000,000 4/15 J.B.C. & A. A.D.S.S./Forms/C. 2118.

Vol. 27

War Diary.

13th Battalion Royal Welch Fusrs.

February 1918.

27 B

Army Form C. 2118

Instructions regarding War Diaries and Intelligence Summaries are contained in F. S. Regs., Part II. and the Staff Manual respectively. Title Pages will be prepared in manuscript.

WAR DIARY
or
INTELLIGENCE SUMMARY
(Erase heading not required.)

FEBURARY. 1918.

Place	Date	Hour	Summary of Events and Information	Remarks and references to Appendices
[illegible]	[illegible]		[illegible]	

1875 Wt. W593/826 1,000,000 [illegible] J. B. C. & A. A.D.S.S./Forms/C.2118.

Instructions regarding War Diaries and Intelligence Summaries are contained in F. S. Regs., Part II. and the Staff Manual respectively. Title Pages will be prepared in manuscript.

WAR DIARY
or
INTELLIGENCE SUMMARY

(Erase heading not required.)

FEBURARY

Army Form C. 2118

Place	Date	Hour	Summary of Events and Information	Remarks and references to Appendices
In the field	10/2/18		Church parades.	
	11/2/18		Baths. Training, gas drill, inspection of S. B. Rs. Battalion Musketry Competition on 30 yds range. Best section 'C' Coy. Best No 1 & 2 Lewis gun 'C' Coy. Runners Competition A Coy. Stretcher bearers Competition 'C' Coy. Best turned out Cooker 'D' Coy. Transport Competitions (Battalion) Best turned out officers Charger: Adjutants. Best Turned out pair of mules. Best Pack mule.	
	12/2/18.		Training as per programme. Brigade Boxing Competition between 13 & 16th Royal Welch Fus.	
	13/2/18		Battalion proceeded by line march route, staging night 13/14th Feb. at Berquette. S.B.Rs worn for 15 minutes.	
	14/2/18.		Battalion moved to ESTAIRES by line of march route. S.B.Rs worn for 20 minutes.	
	15/2/18.		Baths, special foot treatment. Battalion relieved the 9th Battalion Kings Liverpools in the ARMENTIERES Sector.	

[signature] Major, Cmdg 13th R.W. Fus.

1875 Wt. W593/826 1,000,000 4/15 J.B.C. & A. A.D.S.S./Forms/C. 2118.

Instructions regarding War Diaries and Intelligence Summaries are contained in F. S. Regs., Part II. and the Staff Manual respectively. Title Pages will be prepared in manuscript.

Army Form C. 2118

WAR DIARY
or
INTELLIGENCE SUMMARY

(Erase heading not required.)

FEBRUARY 1918

Place	Date	Hour	Summary of Events and Information	Remarks and references to Appendices
In the field	15/2/18 (cont)		Dispositions after relief "C" Coy RIGHT front. D Coy LEFT front. A Coy RIGHT Support B Coy (Garrison Coy) LEFT Support. Relief Complete 8.0 pm.	[illegible] Major Comdg. 13th R.W. Fus.
	16/2/18		Hostile artillery active. A good deal of movement heard in enemy lines during night. One patrol sent out.	
	17/2/18		Enemy artillery very active, about 1000 shells on NOUVEAU HOUPLINES. Patrols sent out at night.	
	18/2/18		Hostile artillery active. Support line shelled at intervals. ARMENTIÈRES shelled with gas shells.	
	19/2/18		16th Royal Welsh Fus. relieved the 13th Battn. ARMENTIÈRES Section. Battalion moved into reserve at WATERLANDS CAMP. All in billets by 11.0 pm.	
	20/2/18		Baths.	

1875 Wt. W593/826 1,000,000 4/15 J.B.C. & A. A.D.S.S./Forms/C. 2118.

Instructions regarding War Diaries and Intelligence Summaries are contained in F. S. Regs., Part II. and the Staff Manual respectively. Title Pages will be prepared in manuscript.

WAR DIARY
or
INTELLIGENCE SUMMARY
(Erase heading not required.)

Army Form C. 2118

FEBRUARY 1918

Place	Date	Hour	Summary of Events and Information	Remarks and references to Appendices
In the field	21/2/18		Working parties. Inspection of Gas helmets by Bde. Gas Officer	[illegible] Major Cmdg 13th R.W. Fus.
	22/2/18		B Coy move from Waterlands into billets at ERQUINGHEM, all in billets at 12.30 p.m.	
"	23/2/18		Battalion less B Coy, moved to billets in ERQUINGHEM all in billets by 12.30 p.m.	
"	24/2/18		Training under company arrangements. Battalion moved into Support at ARMENTIERES all in billets by 6.0 p.m. C Coy in SUBSIDIARY LINE.	
"	25/2/18		Working parties.	
"	26/2/18		Baths.	
"	27/2/18		13th Royal Welch Fus. relieved 14th Royal Welch Fus. in ARMENTIERES Section dispositions B Coy LEFT. FRONT. A. " RIGHT " D " LEFT. SUPPORT. C " RIGHT " Relief complete 8.45 p.m.	

1875 Wt. W593/826 1,000,000 4/15 J.B.C. & A. A.D.S.S./Forms/C. 2118.

Instructions regarding War Diaries and Intelligence Summaries are contained in F. S. Regs., Part II. and the Staff Manual respectively. Title Pages will be prepared in manuscript.

WAR DIARY
or
INTELLIGENCE SUMMARY
(Erase heading not required.)

Army Form C. 2118

FEBRUARY 1918

Place	Date	Hour	Summary of Events and Information	Remarks and references to Appendices

1875 Wt. W593/826 1,000,000 [illegible] & A. A.D.S.S./Forms/C. 2118.

Vol 28

13TH BATTN ROYAL WELSH FUSILIERS

WAR DIARY

FOR

MARCH - 1918

28B
5 sheets

Instructions regarding War Diaries and Intelligence Summaries are contained in F. S. Regs., Part II. and the Staff Manual respectively. Title pages will be prepared in manuscript.

Army Form C. 2118.

WAR DIARY
or
INTELLIGENCE SUMMARY.
(Erase heading not required.)

MARCH 1918

Place	Date	Hour	Summary of Events and Information	Remarks and references to Appendices
	1/3/18		Day quiet except for the shelling of enemy T.M. positions by Heavy guns from 6 pm to 9 pm. all our guns were very active. At 9 pm artillery fire died out.	J. H. [illegible] Lt Col. Commanding 13 R.W.F.
	2/3/18		Day quiet expect for activity on part of our T. Ms who shelled enemy wire during afternoon.	
	3/3/18		At 12 midnight heavy barrage on enemy front & support lines. 12.10 Enemy shelled our lines, also sent over Gas shells into CHAPPEL ARMENTIÈRES. At 3.15 am a small hostile patrol approach one of our posts but were driven off by the garrison. Relieved by 14 R.W.F. Battalion moved into Support in ARMENTIÈRES. All in billets by 9 pm.	
	4/3/18		Battalion in rest. Working parties.	
	5/3/18		Baths, working parties.	
	6/3/18		Working parties and Baths.	
	7/3/18		Working parties.	
	8/3/18		do	
	9/3/18		Relieved the 14th Battn in the front line trench ARMENTIÈRES Section	

2353 Wt. W2544/1454 700,000 5/15 D. D. & L. A.D.S.S./Forms/C. 2118.

Instructions regarding War Diaries and Intelligence Summaries are contained in F. S. Regs., Part II. and the Staff Manual respectively. Title Pages will be prepared in manuscript.

WAR DIARY
or
INTELLIGENCE SUMMARY
(Erase heading not required.)

Army Form C. 2118

Place	Date	Hour	Summary of Events and Information	Remarks and references to Appendices
			Dispositions R. Front Coy. C Coy R Subsidiary Coy A Coy. L. Front Coy D Coy L Subsidiary Coy B Coy. Relief Complete 9.45 p.m.	
	10/3/18		During early hours of the morning enemy raided our left company under cover of a very heavy barrage. Several men were killed and a few missing enemy casualties unknown.	
	11/3/18		Hostile artillery active during day. Patrols sent out at night.	
	12/3/18		Quiet day. Posts wired during night.	
	13/3/18		Day quiet. Subsidiary line companies relieved front line companies.	
	14/3/18		Our Artillery active cutting wire cutting in front of INCANDESCANT TRENCH.	
	15/3/18		Wire cutting by our artillery during day. 10pm. 16th RWF carried out a raid on the battalion front. 13 Prisoners & two MGs were secured.	
	16/3/18		Quiet day. 13th Bat Relieved by the 16 Battn R.W.F. in the ARMENTIÈRES Section Battalion moved into Bde rest in ERQUINGHEM. All in billets by 11.15pm	
	17/3/18		Several H.V. shells fell in ERQUINGHEM. Battalion moved into ARMENTIÈRES all in billets by 8.30pm.	
	18/3/18		Working parties and Baths.	

J. F. Leman Lt Col.
Commanding 13th R.W.F.

1875 Wt. W593/826 1,000,000 4/15 J.B.C. & A. A.D.S.S./Forms/C. 2118.

Instructions regarding War Diaries and Intelligence Summaries are contained in F. S. Regs., Part II. and the Staff Manual respectively. Title Pages will be prepared in manuscript.

WAR DIARY
or
INTELLIGENCE SUMMARY
(Erase heading not required.)

Army Form C. 2118

MARCH 1918.

Place	Date	Hour	Summary of Events and Information	Remarks and references to Appendices
	19/3/18		Working parties	
	20/3/18		Battalion relieved the 14th R.W.F. in Support. Relief complete 10.30 pm. dispositions B Coy + H.Q.s at the ASYLUM. 'C' Coy BRICKSTACKS. A + D Coy SACRE COEUR cellars.	
	21/3/18		Heavy gas shell attack from 5.20 till 7.30 am.	
	22/3/18		Working parties.	
	23/3/18		Working parties	
	24/3/18		Relieved 14th Battalion R.W.F in front line ARMENTIERES SECTOR. relief complete 11 pm. dispositions A Coy Right Subsidiary Line B Coy Left Subsidiary Line, 'C' Right front Company. D Coy Left ~~Right~~ front Company	
	25/3/18		Quiet day. patrols at night	
	26/3/18		Quiet day. Left companies 1st RWF relieved by 13th Welch relief complete 10 pm.	
	27/3/18		11th Battn RWF relieved 13th RWF on Right front relief complete 3 am. Battalion withdrew into Corps reserve at LA ROLANDRIE FARM	J. H. Hemings. Lt-Col Commanding 10th RWF.

1875 Wt. W593/826 1,000,000 4/15 J.B.C. & A. A.D.S.S./Forms/C. 2118

Instructions regarding War Diaries and Intelligence Summaries are contained in F. S. Regs., Part II. and the Staff Manual respectively. Title Pages will be prepared in manuscript.

WAR DIARY
or
INTELLIGENCE SUMMARY
(Erase heading not required.)

Army Form C. 2118

MARCH 1918.

Place	Date	Hour	Summary of Events and Information	Remarks and references to Appendices
IN THE FIELD	28-3-18		Inspections. Baths, Working parties.	
" " "	29.3.18		Church Parade, The 11th Suffolks relieves the 13th R.W.F. at LA ROLANDRIE Relief complete at 2.30pm. Battalion marches to Billets @ NEUF BERQUIN. All in Billets at 7.30 pm.	
" " "	30.3.18		Companies at disposal of Company Commanders, Battalion marches to Billets at LE PARC, Left NEUF BERQUIN at 1.30 pm, all in Billets at LE PARC at 4.30 pm.	
" " "	31.3.18		Inspections, Church Parades morning and evening.	

J. F. Leman. Lt Col
Commanding 13th R.W.F.

1875 Wt. W593/826 1,000,000 4/15 J.B.C. & A. A.D.S.S./Forms/C. 2118.

113th Inf.Bde.
38th Div.

13th BATTN. THE ROYAL WELCH FUSILIERS.

A P R I L

1 9 1 8

13/38

13th Battalion. R W Fus

Vol 29

War Diary

April 1918

E.H.

29B
10 sheets

Instructions regarding War Diaries and Intelligence Summaries are contained in F. S. Regs., Part II. and the Staff Manual respectively. Title Pages will be prepared in manuscript.

WAR DIARY
or
INTELLIGENCE SUMMARY
(Erase heading not required.)

Army Form C. 2118

APRIL 1918.

Place	Date	Hour	Summary of Events and Information	Remarks and references to Appendices
IN THE FIELD	1/4/18.		The Battalion moved from Billets at LE PARC and marched to RLY STN at STEENBECQUE. at 1130 am. (C Coy at 2.30 pm) where it entrained. Detrained at DOULLENS at 9.0 pm. Marched to Billets at HERISSART via SARTON. arrived HERISSART at 4.0 am (C Coy at 6.0 am 2nd inst.)	
"	2/4/18		Left Billets at HERISSART at 2.30 pm for FORCEVILLE. arr in Billets at 6.30 pm.	
"	3/4/18		Received orders to leave FORCEVILLE at 2.0 am. 113th Infantry Bde. marched to HERISSART at 8.30 am. arrived at 12 noon.	
"	4/4/18		[illegible] Coys at disposal of Company Commanders. Projected Brigade Counter attack Scheme postponed owing to bad weather.	
"	5/4/18		Projected Brigade Scheme again postponed. Coys at disposal of Coy Commanders for training and Inspections. The Battalion moved at short notice at 12.30 pm to CONTAY and then on to VADENCOURT. arrived at VADENCOURT at 2.30 pm. Battle Surplus left at 6.0 pm for Billets at TOUTENCOURT. Battalion bivouaked at VADENCOURT for night.	

1875 Wt. W593/826 1,000,000 4/15 J.B.C. & A. A.D.S.S./Forms/C. 2118.

Instructions regarding War Diaries and Intelligence Summaries are contained in F. S. Regs., Part II. and the Staff Manual respectively. Title Pages will be prepared in manuscript.

WAR DIARY
or
INTELLIGENCE SUMMARY
(Erase heading not required.)

Army Form C. 2118

APRIL 1918.

Place	Date	Hour	Summary of Events and Information	Remarks and references to Appendices
In the field	5/4/18	CONTD.	under Brigade arrangements. Counter-attack positions reconnoitred by CO. and Company Commanders.	
	6/4/18		Battalion moved to Billets in PIERREGOT, leaving at 5.0 pm. Battle Surplus left TOUTENCOURT at 4.0 pm. All in Billets at 8.10 pm.	
	7/4/18		Church Parade, Baths. (Special road reconnaissance to CORBIE and return via DAOURS)	
	8/4/18		113th Infantry Bgde Outpost scheme.	
	9/4/18		113th Infantry Bde Counter attack scheme, followed by Outpost scheme.	
	10/4/18		Battalion marched to HARPONVILLE to ~~[illegible]~~ tents. Inspection	
	11/4/18		Battalion ~~[illegible]~~ moved to Forward area, relieving ~~the~~ 6th Queens 37th Bde Sheet 57D. ~~[illegible]~~ EAST of line W21.a.7.6 Battalion HQ at W.26.C.4.8 Dispositions after relief. 'A' Coy Right Front; 'B' Coy Left Front 'C' Coy Right Subsidiary; 'D' Coy Left Subsidiary; 16th Batt R.W.F. on our Left. Relief complete at 3.30am 12/4/18. Battle Surplus proceeded to Billets at CONTAY	Lt Col. [illegible]

1875 Wt. W593/826 1,000,000 4/15 J.B.C. & A. A.D.S.S./Forms/C. 2118.

Instructions regarding War Diaries and Intelligence Summaries are contained in F. S. Regs., Part II. and the Staff Manual respectively. Title Pages will be prepared in manuscript.

WAR DIARY
or
INTELLIGENCE SUMMARY
(Erase heading not required.)

Army Form C. 2118

APRIL 1918

Place	Date	Hour	Summary of Events and Information	Remarks and references to Appendices
In the field	12/4/18		Cloudy, visibility fair. Enemy artillery fairly active on BOUZINCOURT & back areas. Counter battery work. Great aerial activity. Wiring front line by night.	
" "	13/4/18		Enemy & our artillery active. Counter battery work. Aerial activity great. Visibility good.	
" "	14/4/18		Our artillery normal during day but intense on ALBERT at night. At 10 pm an outbreak of fire in ALBERT until 11.30 pm. Enemy snipers more active. M.G. fire moderate. Wiring our line at night.	
" "	15/4/18		Our artillery very active on ALBERT. Our snipers kept enemy movement down. Enemy artillery more active. E.M.Gs active. Wiring our line at night. [illegible] relieved 16th [illegible] on left of [illegible].	
" "	16/4/18		Our artillery active on ALBERT & enemy back areas. Direct hit on Church spire at 3.30 pm brought down the [illegible]. E.A. more active. Enemy artillery quiet. E.M.Gs active. Wiring our front line by night. 12th H.L.I. relieved [illegible] Royal Scots on our right.	
" "	17/4/18		Our artillery active on BOUZINCOURT–ALBERT Road. M.Gs inactive. Aerial activity great. Hostile artillery less active. M.Gs inactive except at night. Wiring at night in front of our line & in front of [illegible].	

1875 Wt. W593/826 1,000,000 4/17 J.B.C. & A. A.D.S.S./Forms/C. 2118.

Army Form C. 2118

Instructions regarding War Diaries and Intelligence Summaries are contained in F. S. Regs., Part II. and the Staff Manual respectively. Title Pages will be prepared in manuscript.

WAR DIARY
or
INTELLIGENCE SUMMARY APRIL 1918
(Erase heading not required.)

Place	Date	Hour	Summary of Events and Information	Remarks and references to Appendices
In the field	18/4/18		Usual artillery activity & aerial activity. nothing unusual happened. During period 12/4/18 to 18/4/18. Work of digging in, consolidating & improving lines proceeded. Patrols were sent out nightly on all parts of our front. Battle Surplus at CONTAY, under Brigade arrangements for special training in L.G.s &c.	
			The 113th Bde, relieved by 115th Bde, 2nd Bn RWF relieving 13th RWF. 13th RWF moved to bivouacs at V.28 b. 60. 45 (Sheet 57 D) Route via BOUZINCOURT – MILLENCOURT. Relief complete @ 12 30 am 19/4/18.	
" "	19/4/18		Cleaning up & inspections &c. Battalion moved to new Bivouacs at V.21 C. 5. 5.	
" "	20/4/18		Attack Scheme by 113th Bde	
" "	21/4/18		" " " " ". 13th RWF proceeded to line relieving 2nd Bn RWF. Dispositions after relief:- Left Front "A" Coy W15.a.20.00 to W15.a.40.70. Centre Front "C" Coy, W15.C.20.99. to W21.a.40.90. Right Front, "D" Coy. W.21.a.40.90 to W21.b.10.20. "B" Coy in Support at W21.a.50.20 to W.21.C.62.80; Sheet 57 D Relief complete at 2 30 a.m. about 10 Casualties during relief by Shells & Gas.	J. F. [illegible] Lt. Col.

1875 Wt. W593/826 1,000,000 4/15 J.B.C. & A. A.D.S.S./Forms/C. 2118.

Army Form C. 2118.

WAR DIARY
or
INTELLIGENCE SUMMARY.
(Erase heading not required.)

APRIL 1918.

Instructions regarding War Diaries and Intelligence Summaries are contained in F. S. Regs., Part II. and the Staff Manual respectively. Title pages will be prepared in manuscript.

Place	Date	Hour	Summary of Events and Information	Remarks and references to Appendices
[illegible]			Great aerial activity. Visibility good. Usual artillery activity. Attack planned to commence at 7.30 pm. Object to capture high ground W 21 Central N.E. to W 21 b. 20.50 and due North to W15 d. 45.45 (line of shell holes) between (?) Right Coy (D Coy) W 21 Central to W 15 d. 45.00 (1 platoon) W 21 Central to W 15 d. 99.00 (2 platoons)	
			Centre Coy (C Coy) W 15 d. 45.00 to W 15 d. 45.25 (1 platoon); Enemy 2nd & 3rd lines W 15 d. 99.10 to W 15 d. 99.30 (2 platoons).	
			Left Coy (A Coy) Enemy First line, W 15 d. 45.25 to W 15 d. 45.45 (1 platoon) Enemy 2nd & 3rd lines, W 15 d. 99.00 to W 15 d. 99.50 (2 platoons)	
			Reserve Coy (B Coy) W 21 b. 40.45 to W 15 d. 45.00 (one platoon) W 21 b. 75.60 to W 15 d. 99.00 (two platoons in [illegible]) This Coy was to keep touch with Right & Centre Coys and fill up gaps by pushing up (?).	
			Sections moved in file until objective which was to be reached. S.O.S. rifle grenade Red Green Red. RAP at W [illegible] Collecting Station at W 15 b. [illegible] [illegible]	

2353 Wt. W2544/1454 700,000 5/15 D. D. & L. A.D.S.S. Forms/C. 2118.

Instructions regarding War Diaries and Intelligence Summaries are contained in F. S. Regs., Part II. and the Staff Manual respectively. Title pages will be prepared in manuscript.

WAR DIARY or INTELLIGENCE SUMMARY.

(Erase heading not required.)

APRIL 1918

Army Form C. 2118.

Place	Date	Hour	Summary of Events and Information	Remarks and references to Appendices
In the field.	25/4/18.	Contd	were carried into attack + 2 LG were kept in reserve at BHQ. @ W14b. 35.50. 18 Pdr Barrage 100x every 3 mins. pause for 3 minutes after 1st objective. Dress F.O. 1 days rtns, 170 rds SAA per man. 2 bombs per NCO + man. 1 aeroplane flare per man. Each section 2 "P" bombs and 1 large wire cutter. Tools 1 pick + 3 shovels per every 4 men. "Very" Pistols were carried + 12 Green Very lights per Coy. Exceedingly heavy M.G. fire was experienced immediately attack commenced. Our heavy guns firing short. The whole attacking forces were considerably held up + heavy casualties received. Hand to hand fighting took place in which much bayonetting was done + severe casualties inflicted on enemy. Progress was slow, after 1st objective taken at zero + 10 minutes. Enemy barrage behind our Support line, a lot of shrapnel bursting high. Much smoke on front line. D Coy reported on ridge at zero + 10. A.C + B. Coys held up by M.G fire. At zero + 20 enemy barrage on ridge holding up advance. At Zero + 29 "A" Coy at first objective. Enemy M.G fire less intense. Enemy	J. H. [illegible] Lt Col.

2353 Wt. W2544/1454 700,000 5/15 D. D. & L. A.D.S.S. Forms/C. 2118.

Instructions regarding War Diaries and Intelligence Summaries are contained in F. S. Regs., Part II. and the Staff Manual respectively. Title pages will be prepared in manuscript.

Army Form C. 2118.

WAR DIARY
or
INTELLIGENCE SUMMARY.
(Erase heading not required.)

APRIL 1918

Place	Date	Hour	Summary of Events and Information	Remarks and references to Appendices
[illegible]	[illegible]	[illegible]	barrage in front of our front line. Zero + 87. MG fire coming up centre. At Zero + 99 situation obscure. Barrage still heavy. Zero + 160. Right Coy reached objective & protecting parties sent out. All Coys except "A" reached final objective. But "C" could not hold on & had to fall back to first objective. Consolidation took place on line approximately W 15 a 35.40 thence SE to W 15 d 42.65 then S. to W 21 b 45 35. Prisoners taken 60, M G reported 3 captured also 1 L.G. which was being used against us. Our Casualties heavy. At Zero + 90 artillery activity became normal. M.G. fire active all night	
	[illegible]		E.A. active, flying over our front line, engaged by L.G. Enemy seen bringing up reinforcements from ALBERT. Artillery fired on them. Dispositions confirmed. A Coy W 15 d 37.70 to W 15 d 00.90. C Coy W 15 [illegible] 70 to W 15 c 35.20, B Coy W 15 d 35.20 to W 15 d 60.00 ([illegible] 2nd [illegible] support) W 15 d 60.00 to W 21 b 50.90 D Coy W 21 b 50.90 to W 21 b [illegible] to W 21 b 35.45 [illegible] W 21 [illegible].	

2353 Wt W2544/1454 700,000 5/15 D. D. & L. A.D.S.S. Forms/C 2118.

Instructions regarding War Diaries and Intelligence Summaries are contained in F. S. Regs., Part II. and the Staff Manual respectively. Title pages will be prepared in manuscript.

WAR DIARY
or
INTELLIGENCE SUMMARY.

(*Erase heading not required.*)

Army Form C. 2118.

APRIL 1918

Place	Date	Hour	Summary of Events and Information	Remarks and references to Appendices
[illegible]	24/4/18		at 5.45 am enemy LTM barrage on front line, enemy seen advancing on 200x front opposite W21 b 50 70 and W21 b 55 52. The enemy were dispersed by rifle & LG fire & suffered heavy casualties.	[illegible]
			Total prisoners from 22/4/18 to 24/4/18. 90 (Officers killed 6 wounded 3) 6 LMGs & 1 LG were captured.	
			Our casualties OR 60 killed 2 died of wounds 109 wounded 2 missing 2 shell shock	
" "	25/4/18		Enemy Artillery very active on our back areas. 13th RWF relieved by 10th SWB and 17th RWF. Battalion moved to billets at WARLOY all in billets at 3.30 am	
" "	26/4/18		Baths, inspections. During period 16/4/18 to 26/4/18 Battle Surplus (less 50% sent to Cramont) at Contay ~~under~~ training under Bde arrangements.	[illegible]
" "	27/4/18		Battalion & Battle Surplus moved to billets at MIRVAUX by march route. Congratulated by Brigadier General Officer Commanding, en route, for work done last tour in line. All in billets at 10.30 am. Cleaning up & inspections	
" "	28/4/18		Church Parades, refitting & reorganization. Officers & Sergts [illegible] reading lecture by B.G.O.C	

2353 Wt. W2544/1454 700,000 5/15 D. D. & L. A.D.S.S./Forms/C. 2118.

Army Form C. 2118.

Instructions regarding War Diaries and Intelligence Summaries are contained in F. S. Regs., Part II. and the Staff Manual respectively. Title pages will be prepared in manuscript.

WAR DIARY
or
INTELLIGENCE SUMMARY.
(Erase heading not required.)

APRIL 1918.

Place	Date	Hour	Summary of Events and Information	Remarks and references to Appendices
[illegible]	29th		Bde. [illegible] Coy arrangements. [illegible] L.G. Class commenced.	
"	30th		Training under Coy arrangements. Reconnaissance of Reserve line [illegible] by O.C. Coy Officers.	
			[illegible] Lt Col. Commanding [illegible]	

2353 Wt. W2544/1454 700,000 5/15 D. D. & L. A.D.S.S. Forms/C. 2118.

13 R.W.F.
Vol. 30

WAR DIARY

FOR THE MONTH OF

MAY 1918

13 R.W.F.

30 B
7 sheets

Instructions regarding War Diaries and Intelligence Summaries are contained in F. S. Regs., Part II. and the Staff Manual respectively. Title pages will be prepared in manuscript.

WAR DIARY
or
INTELLIGENCE SUMMARY.
(Erase heading not required.)

MAY 1918.

Army Form C. 2118.

Place	Date	Hour	Summary of Events and Information	Remarks and references to Appendices
FIELD	1/5/18		Training during Battalion rest at MIRVAUX.	
"	2/5/18		Battalion moved, less Battle Surplus to bivouacs at V 5 a Sheet 57 D.	
			Battle Surplus moved to HARPONVILLE. (Brigade Reserve)	
"	3/5/18		Working parties, wiring "PURPLE LINE" by night	
"	4/5/18		" " " " " "	
"	5/5/18		Battalion relieves the 1st "R.W.F." in line in front of BOUZINCOURT. Right Batt. Centre Bde. Relief complete at 1.0 am. 6.5.18. Dispositions after relief:- Left Front "B" Coy; Right Front, "C" Coy; Support "D" Coy. Reserve "A" Coy. B.H.Q. in BOUZINCOURT.	
"	6/5/18		Our artillery very active on enemy back areas & AVELUY WOOD. Our aircraft active. Enemy not quite so active.	
"	7/5/18		At periods our artillery very active, also our aircraft between 5 pm & 8 pm. Enemy active at times. M.G. very active. No E.A. seen.	
"	8/5/18		Our artillery active at intervals during day & night. [illegible] Enemy artillery very active at 11.30 pm after having sent up S.O.S. on Batt. right also at 4.0 am.	

[illegible] Major
Commanding [illegible]

2353 Wt. W2544/1451 700,000 5/15 D. D. & L. A.D.S.S. Forms/C 2118.

Army Form C. 2118.

Instructions regarding War Diaries and Intelligence Summaries are contained in F. S. Regs., Part II. and the Staff Manual respectively. Title pages will be prepared in manuscript.

WAR DIARY
or
INTELLIGENCE SUMMARY.
(Erase heading not required.)

MAY 1918.

Place	Date	Hour	Summary of Events and Information	Remarks and references to Appendices
FIELD	9/5/18		Enemy Artillery active during period. at 11.20 to 11.40 pm. an intense bombardment, after enemy S.O.S. sent up on Right of Battalion. BOUZINCOURT also heavily shelled at intervals. Our Artillery very active. Aircraft more active.	
"	10/5/18		Attack by 114th Bde (on our left) on AVELUY WOOD. Both artilleries very active. Bombing + Rifle Grenades from our front line on Y Shaped ravine with good results. Intermittent Shelling during day, but enemy artillery very quiet during night. Inter company relief D Coy relieved B Coy Left Front, A Coy relieves C Coy Right Front. Front Coy H.Q.s removed to SUPPORT LINE. Line held with 4 Platoons in FRONT LINE. 2 Coy H.Q. + 2 Platoons in SUPPORT LINE. 2 Coys in RESERVE LINE.	
"	11/5/18		Nothing unusual happened. Artillery on both sides fairly active.	
"	12/5/18.		BOUZINCOURT heavily shelled by "Crackers" during day + night. at 10.30 pm heavy bombardment of our FRONT + SUPPORT LINES. This was repeated at 4.30am 13.5.18. Aircraft on both sides very active.	

[signature] Major. Commanding 13 R.W.F.

2353 Wt. W2544/1454 700,000 5/15 D. D. & L. A.D.S.S./Forms/C. 2118.

Instructions regarding War Diaries and Intelligence Summaries are contained in F. S. Regs., Part II. and the Staff Manual respectively. Title pages will be prepared in manuscript.

Army Form C. 2118.

WAR DIARY
or
INTELLIGENCE SUMMARY. MAY 1918

(*Erase heading not required.*)

Place	Date	Hour	Summary of Events and Information	Remarks and references to Appendices
FIELD	13/5/18		Usual artillery activity on both sides. 13th Batt R.I.F. relieved by 14th Batt R.I.F. The Batt moved to Bivouacs in V.5 a & d. Sheet 57D. Relief complete at 12.30 am 14/5/18. 2 Coys of 13th R.I.F. in reserve - B Coy at W12 d. 8. 2. C Coy at W 7 b. 10. 50.	[signature] Major Commanding 13th R.I.F.
"	14/5/18		Working parties on new dugouts at V12 c. and new Bde H.Q. at V 5 a	
"	15/5/18		Working parties as above. Enemy registered near Bivouacs at V5 a.	
"	16/5/18		Further registration by enemy on V5 a during afternoon. at 9.30 pm to midnight enemy heavily shelled Bivouacs in V5 a sending over about 400 shells mostly 5.9s. No casualties.	
"	17/5/18		B Coy, C Coy & H.Q. moved to new dug outs in V12 C. at 10.0 am. D Coy relieved B Coy at W12 d 8 2. and A Coy relieved C Coy at W 7 b. 10. 50. Working parties.	
"	18/5/18		Working parties.	
"	19/5/18		Working parties. The 113th Bde relieved by 106th Bde. The 13th Batt	

2353 Wt. W2544/1451 700,000 5/15 D. D. & L. A.D.S.S. Forms/C 2118.

Instructions regarding War Diaries and Intelligence Summaries are contained in F. S. Regs., Part II. and the Staff Manual respectively. Title pages will be prepared in manuscript.

WAR DIARY
or
INTELLIGENCE SUMMARY. MAY 1918
(Erase heading not required.)

Army Form C. 2118.

Place	Date	Hour	Summary of Events and Information	Remarks and references to Appendices
FIELD	19/5/18		RWF relieved by 12th Batt HLI. Relief Complete at 12.0 midnight. On relief Batt proceeded by march route to billets at RUEBOMPRE halting for breakfast at HARPONVILLE. All in billets at 7.30 am 20.5.18	[signature] Major Commanding 13th RWF.
"	20/5/18		Inspections. Cleaning up.	
"	21/5/18		Training according to Brigade Scheme & Batt programme. Baths. Recreation	
"	22/5/18		" " " " " " " "	
"	23/5/18		" " " " " " " "	
"	24/5/18		" " " " " " " "	
"	25/5/18		" " " " " " " "	
"	26/5/18		Brigade Church Parade Service & Recreation in afternoon. Reconnaissance by Officers of ground for Bde attack & Counter attack Scheme.	
"	27/5/18		Training in accordance with programme from 8 am to 11 am. Bde Scheme during afternoon. Attack commenced from Rly S. of TOUTENCOURT attacking high ground between T2 b. 00.50 & T 3 d. 15.30.	

D. D. & L., London, E.C.
(A8094) Wt W1771/M2031 750,000 5/17 Sch. 52 Forms/C2118/14

Instructions regarding War Diaries and Intelligence Summaries are contained in F. S. Regs., Part II. and the Staff Manual respectively. Title pages will be prepared in manuscript.

WAR DIARY
or
INTELLIGENCE SUMMARY.
(Erase heading not required.)

Army Form C. 2118.

May 1918

Place	Date	Hour	Summary of Events and Information	Remarks and references to Appendices
FIELD	27/5/18	[illegible]	Two Battalions i.e. 13th RWF & 14th RWF attacked & the 16th RWF counter-attacked. The Army Commander, the Corps Commander, the Divisional Commander and Brigadier General Commanding witnessed the scheme.	[illegible] Major Commanding 13th RWF
FIELD	28/5/18		Training as per programme. Officers witnessed an attack with Tanks in afternoon. Lecture by B.G.C. to all ranks on AEROPLANE PHOTOS.	
"	29/5/18		Training in accordance with programme.	
"	30/5/18		Rehearsal of Corps Commanders inspection of Bde Group by B.G.C. Baths. Recreation.	
"	31/5/18		Inspection of 113th Brigade Group by Corps Commander. The Battalion was complimented by Corps Commander, Divisional Commander and Brigade Commander on its smart appearance, clean turnout and good drill. Medal ribbons were distributed by the Corps Commander to the following:- M.C. Capt C.B. Williams, 2nd Lt J.P. Hannan, R.S.M. T. Davies. Bar to M.C. 2nd Lt A.C. Ford; D.C.M. Sgt T.L. Jones, Sgt D. Morgan & Cpl R. Humphreys. Croix de Guerre Sgt C.B. Pliner & Corpl J.C. Kirby.	

D. D. & L., London, E.C. (A8 op) Wt W1771/M2031 250,000 5/15 Sch. 52 Forms/C2118/14

Instructions regarding War Diaries and Intelligence Summaries are contained in F. S. Regs., Part II. and the Staff Manual respectively. Title pages will be prepared in manuscript.

WAR DIARY
or
INTELLIGENCE SUMMARY.
(Erase heading not required.)

MAY 1918.

Army Form C. 2118.

Place	Date	Hour	Summary of Events and Information	Remarks and references to Appendices
FIELD	31/5/18	Contd	MMs. Pte R J Jones, Cpl J Thomas, Sgt A. Hoyle. L/Sgt G a Pipping. Cpl J Parcher. Sgt J T Jones Sgt R J Way, L/Sgt E H Jones, Cpl J Williams, Pte R Fish, Pte G Jones, Pte H Owen, Pte H Tyrrell, & Pte Turkington. Bar to MM Sgt. E Westwood.	
			During training Special attention has been given to training of Lewis Gunners. also to Musketry and inspection of S.B.R's and Gas Drill.	
			A Brigade Association Football Competition was held, with the following results. 14th RWF beat Bde HQ by 1 goal to nil; 16th RWF beat 13th RWF by 1 goal to nil, 16th RWF beat 14th RWF by 4 goals to 3. The winners, 16th RWF, were selected to meet a team from the 153rd French Division.	
			[illegible] Major, Commanding 13th R W Fus.	

D. D. & L., London, E.C. (A8004) Wt W1771/M2931 750,000 5/17 Sch. 58 Forms/C2118/14

Vol 31

13th BATT. ROYAL WELSH FUSILIERS.

WAR DIARY

FOR

JUNE 1918.

Army Form C. 2118.

WAR DIARY
or
INTELLIGENCE SUMMARY. JUNE 1918.

(Erase heading not required.)

Instructions regarding War Diaries and Intelligence Summaries are contained in F. S. Regs., Part II. and the Staff Manual respectively. Title pages will be prepared in manuscript.

Place	Date	Hour	Summary of Events and Information	Remarks and references to Appendices
FIELD	1/6/18.		Training as per programme in morning. Battalion sports in afternoon for prizes subscribed by Officers. A huge success.	J. G. Lennon Lt. Col.
"	2/6/18		Church Parades. Divisional Jumping Competition for Officers in afternoon.	
"	3/6/18		Training as per programme in morning. Reconnaissance of MESNIL Sector by C.O. & Company Commanders. Boxing and wrestling Competitions in evening.	
"	4/6/18		Battalion proceeded by march route to ACHEUX WOOD leaving RUBEMPRE at 5.0 pm. Battle Surplus proceeded to CRAMONT. Transport, QM Stores & Details billeted at LEALVILLERS.	
	5/6/18		Battalion took over line relieving ANSON Battalion in the Left (MESNIL NORTH) Section of MESNIL SECTION. Relief complete at 1.00 a.m. on 6/6/18. Dispositions: "B" Coy Left Front, "A" Coy Right Front, "D" Coy Left Support, "C" Coy Right Support.	
	6/6/18 – 9/6/18		Patrols from Front Line Companies covered the Battalion front every night without encountering the enemy.	
	9/6/18		Inter-Company Relief "D" Coy relieving "B" Coy and "C" Coy relieving "A" Coy.	

D. D. & L., London, E.C. (A8504) Wt W1771/M2031 750,000 5/17 Sch. 52 Forms/C2118/14

Instructions regarding War Diaries and Intelligence Summaries are contained in F. S. Regs., Part II. and the Staff Manual respectively. Title pages will be prepared in manuscript.

WAR DIARY
or
INTELLIGENCE SUMMARY.
(Erase heading not required.)

June 1918

Army Form C. 2118.

Place	Date	Hour	Summary of Events and Information	Remarks and references to Appendices
FIELD	5/6/18		Assisted the 17th Division on our left, by firing Coloured Rockets and Lights, Lewis Gun and Rifle fire and the discharge of Rifle Grenades, during a minor operation carried out by them.	
	10/6/18		"D" Coy took over from the 14th R.W. Fus. the front line of the MESNIL Sector from [illegible] ALLEY to DRAKE ALLEY. New Dispositions:- "D" Coy Left front and Support, "A" Coy Centre front and Support, "C" Coy Right front and Support, "B" Coy in Reserve.	
	10/12/6/18		Our Patrols [illegible] our ~~Right~~ Left and Centre Fronts, while patrols of the [illegible] patrolled our Right front during this period. No hostile patrols encountered.	
	13/6/18		The Battalion was relieved in the front line by the 16th R.W. Fus. [illegible] 12 midnight. The eight days spent in the front line were uneventful and quiet.	
			The Battalion moved into [illegible] Support Position. All in Billets 1.30 a.m. on [illegible].	
	14/18/6/18		[illegible] Battalion, less 35, were engaged in digging trenches and [illegible] throughout this period under R.E. arrangements.	
	19/6/18		Enemy [illegible] from 12 midnight to 3.00 a.m. on the 25th and by the Corps Artillery. Very heavy from 2 a.m. to 3 a.m. following a discharge of [illegible] Gas Projectors on the left. Enemy retaliation not heavy.	

D. D. & L. London, E.C.
(A8 op) Wt. W. [illegible] Sch. 52 Forms/C2118/14

Instructions regarding War Diaries and Intelligence Summaries are contained in F. S. Regs., Part II. and the Staff Manual respectively. Title pages will be prepared in manuscript.

WAR DIARY
or
INTELLIGENCE SUMMARY.
(Erase heading not required.)

Army Form C. 2118.

June 1918

Place	Date	Hour	Summary of Events and Information	Remarks and references to Appendices
FIELD	21/6/18		The 2nd R.W.Fus and the 16th R.W.Fus raided the enemy positions on our Right Front and immediate Right. Zero hour 2.00 a.m.	J. H. [illegible] Lt. Col
	22/6/18		2/Lieut A. J. PAGE and 8 O.R. silently raided the enemy post in front of HAMEL. The Raiding party left our Left Front (through the 16th R.W.FUS) at 1.00 a.m. They entered the Post, after cutting three belts of wire at 3.00 a.m but found the Post evacuated by the enemy.	
			The Battalion was relieved by the 2nd R W Fus in Support (Relief complete at 11.00 p.m) and moved into Reserve. All in Billets at 12 30 a.m on 23/6/18	
	23/6/18		Cleaning up and Inspections. Voluntary Church Service in evening	
	24/6/18		Training as per Programme of Training. Battalion, less 35, engaged in improving trenches of Purple System (in front of ENGLEBELMER) at night	
	25/6/18		——— do ——— do ———	
	26/6/18		Tactical Scheme in ACHEUX WOOD	
	27/6/18 } 28/6/18 }		{Training as per Programme of Training, and working parties during {day on Brown System (in front of FORCEVILLE).	
	29/6/18		Tactical Scheme in ACHEUX WOOD	

D. D. & L., London, E.C. (A8094) Wt W1771/M2031 750,000 5/17 Sch. 52 Forms/C2118/14

Army Form C. 2118.

Instructions regarding War Diaries and Intelligence Summaries are contained in F. S. Regs., Part II. and the Staff Manual respectively. Title pages will be prepared in manuscript.

WAR DIARY
or
INTELLIGENCE SUMMARY.
(Erase heading not required.)

June 1918

Place	Date	Hour	Summary of Events and Information	Remarks and references to Appendices
Field	30/6/18		Brigade [illegible] [illegible] Divisional [illegible] in attendance. Commanding Officer and Company Commanders [illegible] AVELUY WOOD SECTOR.	
			End 1st July 1918	
			[illegible] Lieut. Col. Comdg. 13th R W Fus	

D. D. & L., London, E.C. (A6299) Wt. W5432/M1 750,000 5/18 Sch. 52 Forms/C2118/14

13TH BATT. ROYAL WELSH FUSILIERS

Vol 32

WAR DIARY

FOR

JULY 1918

32 B
5 sheets

Instructions regarding War Diaries and Intelligence Summaries are contained in F. S. Regs., Part II. and the Staff Manual respectively. Title pages will be prepared in manuscript.

WAR DIARY
or
INTELLIGENCE SUMMARY.
(Erase heading not required.)

Army Form C. 2118.

Place	Date	Hour	Summary of Events and Information	Remarks and references to Appendices
In Field	1/7/16	–	Day spent in [illegible] fighting kit. At 7 pm Battalion [illegible] near FORCEVILLE & moved up to relieve 2nd Bn R.W.F. in front line, [illegible] sector of the MESNIL sector. Considerable shelling during relief on account of [illegible] raid by the enemy but no casualties. Relief complete 4 am.	[illegible]
" "	2/7/16	–	[illegible] shelling developed considerable intensity about 9.30 am causing several casualties in our right Coy.	
" "	3/7/16	–	Nil.	
" "	4/7/16	–	[illegible]	
" "	5/7/16	–	[illegible] patrols [illegible] enemy post about Q.17.d.36.30 (ref. Sheet 57D S.E. 1/20000.)	
" "	6/7/16	–	[illegible] patrol consisting of 2 offs. & 15 O.R. [illegible] nothing to [illegible]	
" "	7/7/16	–	[illegible] 15th R.W.F. [illegible] 16 R.W.F. [illegible] Relief complete 12.30 am	

D. D. & L., London, E.C. (A8 ep) Wt W[illegible] Sch. 52 Forms/C2118/11

Instructions regarding War Diaries and Intelligence Summaries are contained in F. S. Regs., Part II. and the Staff Manual respectively. Title pages will be prepared in manuscript.

WAR DIARY
or
INTELLIGENCE SUMMARY.
(Erase heading not required.)

Army Form C. 2118.

Place	Date	Hour	Summary of Events and Information	Remarks and references to Appendices
—	Contd.		On completion of relief the 13th R.W.F. moved to position vacated by the 16th R.W.F. in the Intermediate System.	
[illegible]	7/7/18	—	Working - parties in accordance with Bde table.	
"	8/7/18	—	" " " " " " "	
"	9/7/18	—	" " " " " " "	
	10/7/18		" " " " " " "	
	11/7/18		" " " " " " "	
	12/7/18		" " " " " " "	
"	13/7/18	—	The battalion was relieved in the Intermediate System by the 2nd R.W.F. [illegible] complete at 12-30 a.m. On completion of relief the battalion moved to [illegible] in CARDIFF CAMP ([illegible])	
"	[illegible]	—	[illegible]	
			Parades in vicinity of Camp.	
	[illegible]	—	Battalion [illegible] party in [illegible]	
"	16/7/18	—	[illegible] — Parades according to time table.	
"	17/7/18		Parades — training in accordance with time table	J. [illegible]

D. D. & L., London, E.C.
(A8204) Wt W1771/M2031 750,000 5/17 Sch. 52 Forms/C2118/14

Instructions regarding War Diaries and Intelligence Summaries are contained in F. S. Regs., Part II. and the Staff Manual respectively. Title pages will be prepared in manuscript.

WAR DIARY
or
INTELLIGENCE SUMMARY.

(Erase heading not required.)

Army Form C. 2118.

Place	Date	Hour	Summary of Events and Information	Remarks and references to Appendices
[illegible]	[illegible]	—	Training in rear area in [illegible] Time Table.	[illegible]
"	[illegible]	—	" " " " + Batt[n] working party	
			Capt. [illegible] Bateman took command of the battalion vice [illegible] who took command of Brigade (13 Inf) in absence of Brig. Gen. on leave.	
"	[illegible]	—	Battalion working party on Brown System (5.30 am to [illegible] am) Training (2.30 to 4.30 pm).	
	[illegible]	—	Major [illegible] [illegible] command of the [illegible] battalion [illegible] [illegible] [illegible] [illegible] in command.	
			Battalion working party on Brown System (5.30 am to 9.30 am) Training (2.30 pm to 4.30 pm).	
"	[illegible]	—	Battalion working party on Brown System (5.30 am to [illegible]) Training (2.30 pm to [illegible] pm).	
	[illegible]	—	Battalion working party on Brown System (5.30 am to [illegible] am) Training (2.30 pm to [illegible] pm).	
"	[illegible]	—	Battalion working party on Brown System (5.30 am to 9.30 am) Training (2.30 pm to 4.30 pm).	
	[illegible]	—	[illegible] [illegible] [illegible] [illegible] 2 pm to 4 pm Training	

D. D. & L. London, E.C. (A2601) Wt W1771/M2031 750,000 5/16 Sch. 52 Forms/C2118/14

Army Fo[illegible]

Instructions regarding War Diaries and Intelligence Summaries are contained in F. S. Regs., Part II. and the Staff Manual respectively. Title pages will be prepared in manuscript.

WAR DIARY
or
INTELLIGENCE SUMMARY.
(Erase heading not required.)

Place	Date	Hour	Summary of Events and Information	Remarks and references to Appendices
[illegible]	26/7/18	–	Training in accordance with Time-Table (8-30 am to 12-30 am and 2-30 pm to 4-30 pm)	J. [illegible]
"	27/7/18	–	" " " " "	
"	28/7/18	–	Firing on Range and Church Parades.	
"	29/7/18	–	Training in accordance with Time Table. Lt Col Leman resumed command of the Battalion vice Major Sweet who then took up duties as second in Command	
"	30/7/18	–	Morning – Firing on range. Afternoon – Battalion moved by march route to RAINCHEVAL "All in Billets" reported 5.30 pm.	
"	31/7/18	–	Firing on Range near ARQUEVES.	

D. D. & L., London, E.C. (A8004) Wt W1771/M2031 750,000 5/17 Sch. 52 Forms/C2118/14

113/38.

13th Batt Royal Welsh Fusiliers

33

War Diary

For

August 1918

Instructions regarding War Diaries and Intelligence Summaries are contained in F. S. Regs., Part II. and the Staff Manual respectively. Title pages will be prepared in manuscript.

WAR DIARY
or
INTELLIGENCE SUMMARY.
(Erase heading not required.)

August 1918

Army Form C. 2118.

Place	Date	Hour	Summary of Events and Information	Remarks and references to Appendices
In the field	1/8/18	–	Tactical Scheme. – Practice counter-attack on HEDAUVILLE-SWITCH.	[illegible] Major Commanding 13th [illegible]
"	2/8/18	–	" " – Continuation of yesterday's scheme.	
"	3/8/18	–	Morning:– Battalion marched to ARQUEVES to watch demonstration with tracer ammunition. Afternoon: Holiday – Divisional Sports at Herissart.	
"	4/8/18	–	Church Parades.	
		9-30pm	Battalion marched from RAINCHEVAL to HERISSART. All in billets 11-50pm.	
"	5/8/18		Companies at disposal of Company Commanders for inspection prior to proceeding to the line.	
		2-30pm	Demonstration with message-carrying rockets & tracer ammunition	
"	6/8/18	9am	Battalion marched to Cardiff Camp, (FORCEVILLE) & remained there until 8pm.	
		8pm	Moved to the line. 13th Bn R.W.F. relieved the 10th Bn Lancs. Fus. in Left sub-sector of the AVELUY sector. – Four Companies in line & distributed in depth. Four officers of the 1st/315th Amer. Inf. Regt. attached for instruction.	
"	7/8/18	–	Considerable care necessary owing to numerous 'booby traps' left in part of line just evacuated by the enemy.	
"	8/8/18	–	Capt. G. M. Jones M.C. joined Battle Surplus as Adjutant to Divnl. Reception Camp. One Company of 1st Bn/318th Amer. Inf. Regt. attached.	

D. D. & L., London, E.C. (A8004) Wt W1771/M2031 750,000 5/17 Sch. 52 Forms/C2118/14

Army Form C. 2118.

Instructions regarding War Diaries and Intelligence Summaries are contained in F. S. Regs., Part II, and the Staff Manual respectively. Title pages will be prepared in manuscript.

WAR DIARY
or
INTELLIGENCE SUMMARY.

(Erase heading not required.)

August 1918

Place	Date	Hour	Summary of Events and Information	Remarks and references to Appendices
		–	[illegible] B[illegible] Training.	
	[illegible]		[illegible] A+C Coys in front line B+D Coys in support [illegible]	
	[illegible]	–	[illegible] Battn [illegible] ANCRE [illegible]	
	[illegible]	–	[illegible]	
			[illegible]	
		–	[illegible]	
	[illegible]		[illegible]	
	15/8	–	Training	

Instructions regarding War Diaries and Intelligence Summaries are contained in F. S. Regs., Part II. and the Staff Manual respectively. Title pages will be prepared in manuscript.

WAR DIARY
or
INTELLIGENCE SUMMARY.
(*Erase heading not required.*)

Army Form C. 2118.

August 1918

Place	Date	Hour	Summary of Events and Information	Remarks and references to Appendices
In the field	16/8/18	-	Training	[signature] Major Commanding 13th Bn R.W.Fus.
"	17/8/18	-	Morning: Training: Batt. moved from Forceville to Toutencourt. (B Camp & P.O.W. Camp.) All in Billets 7-30 pm.	
"	18/8/18	-	Tactical Scheme: Practice of Advance to occupy an evacuated area. Rehearsal of operation outlined in B.M./S/588.	
"	19/8/18	-	Sports and Recreational Training.	
"	20/8/18	-	Morning: Training: 10-30 pm. Battn. marched from TOUTENCOURT to Brown line near HEDAUVILLE to relieve 13th Bn. Welsh Regt. Relief complete 1 am. (21st Aug.)	
"	21/8/18	-	Training. Lt-Col J. F. Leman went on leave. (one month)	
"	22/8/18	.	8 am. Battalion marched to MELBOURNE COPSE W25a arriving about 12 noon. Parties sent out to reconnoitre roads through ALBERT & bridges across R. ANCRE.	
	23/8/18	.	1.45 am Battalion marched to assembly point at railway cutting E of ALBERT W29a. 4.55 am After preliminary bombardment Bn attacked on a frontage of 2000 yds & carried objectives on a line running from CRUXIFIX CORNER, AVELUY to the ALBERT BAPAUME RD. and consolidated position capturing 2 field guns, 16 MGs, about 150 prisoners & considerable booty. Our casualties: 2/Lieut DAVIES killed; Capts VAUGHAN, C.B WILLIAMS, Lieut H. LEWIS, 2/Lieuts R.B MORGAN & A.J. PAGE wounded. ORs. 20 killed, 117 wounded, 19 missing, 3 gassed. Depth of advance 1800 yds.	

D. D. & L., London, E.C. (A8104) Wt W177/M2031 750,000 5/17 Sch 52 Forms/C2118/14

Instructions regarding War Diaries and Intelligence Summaries are contained in F. S. Regs., Part II. and the Staff Manual respectively. Title pages will be prepared in manuscript.

WAR DIARY
or
INTELLIGENCE SUMMARY.

(Erase heading not required.)

August 1918

Army Form C. 2118.

Place	Date	Hour	Summary of Events and Information	Remarks and references to Appendices
In [illegible]	24/8	[illegible]	Battalion advanced as far as E of LA BOISSELLE X14b following up the 14th & 16th Bns who had carried on the attack through LA BOISSELLE & CONTALMAISON. LT T.W. CONNELL wounded. O.Rs 2 wounded. C Coy was sent to mop up OVILLERS & LA BOISSELLE & reported this village clear of the enemy.	
	25 8/18	2 am	Battalion moved forward towards CONTALMAISON halted in X15b at 9.30 am moved to [illegible] X[illegible] just W. of CONTALMAISON	
		9 pm	Battalion marched to assembly point ~~[illegible]~~ NE of MAMETZ WOOD arriving there [illegible] about 12 midnight. 2 ORs gassed.	
	26/8	[illegible]	After preliminary bombardment ~~[illegible]~~ Battalion launched attack on ~~[illegible]~~ BAZENTIN [illegible] & [illegible] WOOD [illegible] with [illegible] Bns in support & 2nd Bn guarding right flank & mopping up wood. Attack was held up for considerable time by MG fire the wood & village were eventually carried & line advanced to E of village [illegible] S 15 b. 4 OR killed, 27 wounded, 5 missing, 2 gassed.	
	27/8	8 am	The 113 BDE marched on LONGUEVAL without any preliminary artillery fire. The 13th RWF acting as advance guard, B Coy right [illegible] guard & D Coy on the left flank. [illegible] of the village about [illegible] the battalion was held up by [illegible] & [illegible] suffered considerable casualties [illegible] killed; ~~[illegible] killed~~ ~~wounded~~. About 30 prisoners were captured. In the afternoon the Bn [illegible] took up position [illegible] behind the 14th & 16th RWF. Estimated casualties 100	
	28/8		Reconnoitring patrols were sent out [illegible] LONGUEVAL & western edge of DELVILLE WOOD clear of enemy. A & C Coys occupied outpost line in LONGUEVAL VILLAGE. [illegible] wounded.	
	29/8	[illegible]	[illegible] heavy barrage on DELVILLE WOOD.	
			5.45 [illegible] The brigade advanced on GINCHY, 14th & 16th RWF leading with 13th RWF following [illegible] 400 yds behind. GINCHY was reached without [illegible] [illegible] prisoners were taken.	

D. D. & L., London, E.C.
(A8 op) Wt W.[illegible] [illegible] Sch. 52 Forms/C2118/14

Instructions regarding War Diaries and Intelligence Summaries are contained in F. S. Regs., Part II. and the Staff Manual respectively. Title pages will be prepared in manuscript.

WAR DIARY
or
INTELLIGENCE SUMMARY.
(Erase heading not required.)

August 1918

Army Form C. 2118.

Place	Date	Hour	Summary of Events and Information	Remarks and references to Appendices
In the field	30/8/18 } 31/8/18 }		The Batt was the reserve Batt of the reserve Bde. We occupied positions west of GINCHY, and South of DELVILLE WOOD	

[illegible] Major
Cdg 13th Bn [illegible]

D. D. & L., London, E.C.
(A8204) Wt W1771/M2031 750,000 5/17 Sch. 52 Forms/C2118/14

WAR DIARY

for

September 1918.

13th. Batt. ROYAL WELSH FUSILIERS.

Instructions regarding War Diaries and Intelligence Summaries are contained in F. S. Regs., Part II. and the Staff Manual respectively. Title pages will be prepared in manuscript.

Army Form C. 2118.

WAR DIARY
or
INTELLIGENCE SUMMARY.
(*Erase heading not required.*)

September 1918

Place	Date	Hour	Summary of Events and Information	Remarks and references to Appendices
In the field	1/9/18	2.30.am	Battalion marched to assembly point in T.10.c (sunken road behind MORVAL) arriving there at about 4.30. am.	
		4.45am	After preliminary bombardment the 114 Bde and 115 Bde attacked MORVAL with the 113 Bde following in support the 13th R.W.F. being on the left behind the 14th Welsh advancing on a front of 400 yds D Coy on right A Coy on left B Coy in support C Coy being detailed to mop up the village.	
			After some opposition the village was captured and at 6.a.m a line was taken up in the trench EAST of the village at T.11.a, b & c where the 114 Bde was relieved by the 113 Bde the 16th R.W.F. being on the right and the 13th on the left the dividing line being MORVAL - SAILLY. SAILLISEL ROAD - Battalion HQ established in sunken road at T.10.a.8.5. A few prisoners were taken. 2/Lt E. Brash wounded.	
		10.30.am	Our new positions heavily shelled. Enemy reported to be massing in NORTH COPSE U.17.b and QUARRY U.13.a and on ridge in T.12 & T.18 for counterattack. Fired on by our Artillery.	
		1.p.m.	Situation reported quiet.	
		6.30.pm.	113 Bde assembled in T.12b & T.18.a preparatory to attack on SAILLY - SAILLISEL	

D. D. & L., London, E.C.
(A8094) Wt W1771/M2031 750,000 5/17 Sch. 52 Forms/C2118/14

Instructions regarding War Diaries and Intelligence Summaries are contained in F. S. Regs., Part II. and the Staff Manual respectively. Title pages will be prepared in manuscript.

WAR DIARY
or
INTELLIGENCE SUMMARY. September 1918

(Erase heading not required.)

Army Form C. 2118.

Place	Date	Hour	Summary of Events and Information	Remarks and references to Appendices
In the field	1/9/18		Objective - trenches EAST of village in U.8.b & d. - 16th RWF on the right 13th on left Each 500 yds front. Dividing line between Battalions - grid line between T.12 & T.18 14th R.W.F in support.	
		7 p.m.	113 Bde followed creeping barrage. 13 RWF disposed as follows - A Coy left C Coy centre D Coy right B. Coy in support.	
		8 p.m.	SAILLY-SAILLISEL occupied without opposition and line established E of village in U.8.b & d. 13 RWF holding from U.8.d 0.6 to NORTH of village. Batt Hq established at U.8.a.8.1. Casualties Lt. T.S. Bordacs - 2/Lt. N.S. Barlow 2Lt R.H. Ellis wounded. OR killed 7. Wounded 30. Missing 16.	
	2/9/18	3 p.m.	115 Bde passed through 113 Bde under a creeping barrage with the object of taking LE MESNIL en ARROUAISE the 113 Bde being under orders to follow in support of the 115 Bde. The 115 Bde however was held up by heavy M.G. fire and the 113 Bde remained in its original position	
		9 p.m.	A strong counterattack on our left flank was reported to be in preparation	

(Wt. W1 ... Sch. 52 Forms/C2118/14)

Instructions regarding War Diaries and Intelligence Summaries are contained in F. S. Regs., Part II. and the Staff Manual respectively. Title pages will be prepared in manuscript.

WAR DIARY
or
~~INTELLIGENCE SUMMARY.~~
(Erase heading not required.)

September 1918

Army Form C. 2118.

Place	Date	Hour	Summary of Events and Information	Remarks and references to Appendices
In the field	2/9/18		and the 13 RWF took up a position in U.1.D and U.8.a in readiness to attack the enemy's right flank - The counterattack however did not develop and the Batt remained for the night in the position it had taken up.	
			Casualties Lt Palmer wounded. OR. killed 5 - wounded 10.	
	3/9/18	8.3.am	ROCQUIGNY having been taken by the 17th Div. the following patrols backed by Coys were sent out by the 13 RWF. B. Coy to road U.3.a - C Coy to road U.3.c. D Coy to road U.9.a - No sign of the enemy was found.	
		2pm	Advance on MESNIL en ARROUAISE continued 113 Bde on the left 115 Bde on right - 13th RWF on left of 113 Bde 14th on right 16th in support - Dividing line between Batts N. Edge of COPSE in U.3.c and S. Edge of VILLAGE - Objective Trench line U.11. central to U.5.a.60.99.	
			13th RWF assembled on road U.3 a & c. B. Coy on right front - C Coy left front D Coy right supp. A Coy left supp.	
		3.15pm	Objectives reached without opposition	

D. D. & L., London, E.C.
(A8304) Wt W1771/M2031 750,000 5/17 Sch. 52 Forms/C2118/14

Army Form C. 2118.

WAR DIARY
or
INTELLIGENCE SUMMARY. September 1918
(Erase heading not required.)

Instructions regarding War Diaries and Intelligence Summaries are contained in F. S. Regs., Part II. and the Staff Manual respectively. Title pages will be prepared in manuscript.

Place	Date	Hour	Summary of Events and Information	Remarks and references to Appendices
[illegible]	3/9/18		Coy took up position as detailed in the order given above.	
		[illegible]	[illegible] took over position of 14th [illegible] and [illegible] the following [illegible] A.D.C. [illegible] Coy [illegible] 500 [illegible]	
			Casualties [illegible] O.R. killed 3 wounded 6 missing 3	
	4/9/18		[illegible] position taken up on the 3rd	
	5/9/18		[illegible]	
		[illegible]	12th [illegible] EAST of [illegible]	
			[illegible]	
	6/9/18 7/9/18		[illegible]	
	8/9/18		[illegible]	
		[illegible]	[illegible]	
	9/9/18		[illegible]	

D. D. & L., London, E.C. Sch. 52 Forms/C2118/14

Army Form C. 2118.

Instructions regarding War Diaries and Intelligence Summaries are contained in F. S. Regs., Part II. and the Staff Manual respectively. Title pages will be prepared in manuscript.

WAR DIARY
or
~~INTELLIGENCE SUMMARY.~~ September

(*Erase heading not required.*)

Place	Date	Hour	Summary of Events and Information	Remarks and references to Appendices
In the field	10/9/18		38th Div. relieved 17th Div. in the line.	
		2.45 pm	113 Bde marched via GINCHY. LES BOEUFS – LE TRANSLOY to ROCQUIGNY 13th RWF leading.	
		6.30 pm	Arrived ROCQUIGNY where the battn remained for the night.	
	11/9/18		113 Bde relieved 51st Bde in support.	
		8. a.m.	One Officer per Coy and one Hq. Officer proceeded to Q.32.d to reconnoitre new line to be taken over by 13 RWF	
		5.30 pm	13th R.W.F. under the command of Capt. Jones Bateman marched to Q.32.d. and relieved 7th Lincolns	
		9.35 pm	Relief reported complete. Night passed uneventfully.	
	12/9/18 } 13/9/18 }		Situation quiet.	
	14/9/18	1.am	Batt heavily shelled with gas. 48 cases passed through the R.A.P.	
	15/9/18		Day passed uneventfully.	
	16/9/18	7.30 pm	13th R.W.F relieved 10th S.W.B. in the front line from C.T at Q.35.c.1.8 exclusive to E & W grid line between Q.29 and Q.35 and in addition took over from 2nd K.O.S.B from grid line mentioned to Q.28.d.9.5. The Batt. front extended from C.T. at Q.35.c.1.8 exclusive to Q.28.d.9.5. Disposition of Coys. A. on right from C.T. — Q.35.a.2.5. B on left " C T at Q.35.a.2.5 to ~~grid line Q.29 & Q.35~~. Q.28.d.9.5 C & D in support in trench Q.34 b.5.9 — Q.34.a.5.1. Batt Hq. at Q.34.a.3.5.	

D. D. & L., London, E.C.
(A8204) Wt W1771/M2031 750,000 5/17 Sch. 52 Forms/C2118/14

Army Form C. 2118.

WAR DIARY
or
INTELLIGENCE SUMMARY.
(Erase heading not required.)

September

Instructions regarding War Diaries and Intelligence Summaries are contained in F. S. Regs., Part II. and the Staff Manual respectively. Title pages will be prepared in manuscript.

Place	Date	Hour	Summary of Events and Information	Remarks and references to Appendices
[illegible]	1/9/18		Relief was not [illegible] by the enemy	
		[illegible]	Relief reported complete.	
	[illegible]	[illegible]	[illegible] patrols [illegible] to ascertain whether AFRICAN TR. was held by the enemy as it had been reported that there was a possibility of their having withdrawn. AFRICAN TR. was found [illegible] normally.	
			[illegible] Artillery and [illegible] fire.	
"	[illegible]	[illegible]	A [illegible] artillery & T.M. barrage was opened on the enemy's front system of trenches. At the same time, in [illegible] with the troops operating on the flanks the 14th & 16th Bns R.W.F. launched an attack on the enemy's front trench. 13th Bn R.W.F. remained [illegible] our own front line [illegible] the [illegible] [illegible] in Q 34.c. Strongly posted machine gun nests were encountered by the assaulting waves [illegible] suffered heavy casualties & on the left had to retire to [illegible] line. The enemy counter barrage was not very heavy & our own casualties during [illegible] phase of the attack were very slight.	Map Ref. 57c.S.E. 1/20,000
		[illegible]	[illegible] Q 35.c 30.50 [illegible] [illegible] bombardment was placed on AFRICAN TR & machine gun nests at Q 35.c 5.5. [illegible] of bombardment the R.W.F. bombed their way [illegible] AFRICAN TR. [illegible] at Q 35.c 8.8	

D. D. & L., London, E.C.
(A8 0g) Wt. W[illegible] Sch. 52 Forms/C2118/14

Instructions regarding War Diaries and Intelligence Summaries are contained in F. S. Regs., Part II. and the Staff Manual respectively. Title pages will be prepared in manuscript.

WAR DIARY
or
INTELLIGENCE SUMMARY.
(Erase heading not required.)

— September —

Army Form C. 2118.

Place	Date	Hour	Summary of Events and Information	Remarks and references to Appendices
In the field	19/9/18	8pm	13th Bn R.W.F. relieved the 16th Bn. R.W.F. as left front Battalion. After relief the battalion was disposed as follows:—	
			B. Coy. occupying line of posts facing N. & N.E. south of belt of wire running through Q35a sb. & E of AFRICAN TR.	
			C. Coy about junction of C.T. with AFRICAN SUPP. & along C.T. to AFRICAN TR	
			A. Coy from left Bde. boundary at Q29a 0.5 southwards along AFRICAN Support to junction of C.T. with that trench.	
			D. Coy – in reserve near QUEEN'S CROSS.	
	19/9/18	3am	Patrols sent out by B Coy. to establish communication with 2 forward Coys. of 14th R.W.F. but failed to gain touch with them.	
		6.am	Bombing party from B Coy worked along AFRICAN TR. clearing it of the enemy as far N. as Q29a. 8.0.	
		7am	Counter bombing raid was made by the enemy, & owing to lack of bombs & ammunition on the part of our men, succeeded in expelling us from AFRICAN TR. as far S. as Q35c.8.4 thus cutting off with out B Coy who occupied the line of posts in Q35a & b.	
		11am	AFRICAN SUPP. TR. cleared as for concentrated bombardment of yesterday.	
		11-30am	Artillery placed 30 minute bombardment on AFRICAN TR. from Q35a 7.0 to Q29c 95.50	
		12noon	At termination of bombardment 14th R.W.F. attacked with bombing parties	

D. D. & L., London, E.C.
(A8004) Wt W1771/M2031 750,000 5/17 Sch. 52 Forms/C2118/14

Instructions regarding War Diaries and Intelligence Summaries are contained in F. S. Regs., Part II. and the Staff Manual respectively. Title pages will be prepared in manuscript.

WAR DIARY
or
INTELLIGENCE SUMMARY.

(*Erase heading not required.*)

— September —

Army Form C. 2118.

Place	Date	Hour	Summary of Events and Information	Remarks and references to Appendices
		(Continued)		
[illegible]	18/9/18		[illegible] C.T. in Q35c. & up AFRICAN TR. to Q35a central. B & C Coys. 13th R.W.F., with bombing parties attacked along C.T. leading to Q35a central, while A Coy. attacked along the METZ–GOUZEAUCOURT RD. Overcoming determined resistance, the parties of all Companies succeeded in reaching their objectives, [illegible] expelling the enemy from AFRICAN TR as far N as the METZ–GOUZEAUCOURT RD. At the conclusion of the attack the line ran as follows:– AFRICAN SUPP. – C.T. from Q35a 35.55 to Q35a 60.50 – AFRICAN TR to FINS–GOUZEAUCOURT RD. [illegible] [illegible] R.W.F. [illegible] in Q35b.	
		8 pm	Enemy [illegible] remained very [illegible] [illegible] constantly [illegible] of our new positions.	
		[illegible]am.	[illegible] [illegible] uneventfully.	
		4 pm.	The 113th Inf. Bde. was relieved by 2nd R.W.F. & 10th S.W.B., the 2nd R.W.F. [illegible] companies in AFRICAN SUPP. while the 10th S.W.B. [illegible] [illegible] of the Brigade [illegible] E of this line. The relief [illegible] [illegible] by enemy shelling, & was complete [illegible] [illegible] at [illegible] p.m. On completion of relief the battalion moved to reserve [illegible] near DESSART WOOD. Bn. H.Q. [illegible] [illegible] Q32 [illegible] 3.4.	
	[illegible]	8 [illegible]	Battalion [illegible] marched to [illegible] [illegible] in P33, [illegible] [illegible] through P31 [illegible] & Road [illegible] O31 & 35. [illegible] in billets [illegible] 5 pm.	

D. D. & L., London, E.C. (A8 op. Wt. W[illegible] [illegible] Sch. 52 Forms/C2118/14

Instructions regarding War Diaries and Intelligence Summaries are contained in F. S. Regs., Part II. and the Staff Manual respectively. Title pages will be prepared in manuscript.

WAR DIARY
or
INTELLIGENCE SUMMARY.
(*Erase heading not required.*)

— September —

Army Form C. 2118.

Place	Date	Hour	Summary of Events and Information	Remarks and references to Appendices
In the field	–	–	The casualties incurred during the entire operation were:-	† This man was accounted for later — buried by S.W.B.

	Killed	Wounded	Missing	Prisoners
Officers	–	1	–	–
O. Ranks.	12.	44	† 1	* 6

Place	Date	Hour	Summary of Events and Information	Remarks and references to Appendices
			* These men were occupying a post in front of AFRICAN TR. when the latter trench was retaken by the enemy's Counter-bombing raid. They were rushed from behind by superior numbers & forced to surrender.	
	21/9/18	10am to 1pm.	Baths at ROCQUIGNY	
		–	General Cleaning up & inspections	
	22/9/18	–	Church parades.	
	23/9/18	–	Training in accordance with Time-table.	
	24/9/18	–	Lt. Col. Leman, returning from leave, resumed command of the Battn. vice Major Sweet. " " " " "	

D. D. & L., London, E.C.
(A8094) Wt W1771/M2031 750,000 5/17 Sch. 52 Forms/C2118/14

Instructions regarding War Diaries and Intelligence Summaries are contained in F. S. Regs., Part II, and the Staff Manual respectively. Title pages will be prepared in manuscript.

WAR DIARY
or
INTELLIGENCE SUMMARY.

(Erase heading not required.)

— September —

Army Form C. 2118.

Place	Date	Hour	Summary of Events and Information	Remarks and references to Appendices
[illegible]	25th	—	[illegible] according to Time-table.	
			" " " " [illegible] Range.	
	26th	—	" " " "	
	27th		[illegible] [illegible] & [illegible] [illegible], [illegible] by C.O.	
			[illegible] : [illegible] of Brigade [illegible].	
			[illegible] : Battalion Concert.	
	28th		[illegible] : [illegible] & [illegible] [illegible].	
	—	[illegible]	Batt. [illegible] to HEUDECOURT area (W.30 a.) [illegible] [illegible] [illegible] in [illegible]	
			[illegible] [illegible] to Battalion [illegible] in [illegible]	
	29th	—	HEUDECOURT AREA	

[illegible signature]

D. D. & L., London, E.C. (A 7 ep) Wt. W. [illegible] Sch. 52 Forms/C.2118/14.

Vol 35

13th R.W.F.

WAR DIARY FOR OCTOBER

1918

35B
9 sheets

Instructions regarding War Diaries and Intelligence Summaries are contained in F. S. Regs., Part II. and the Staff Manual respectively. Title pages will be prepared in manuscript.

WAR DIARY
or
INTELLIGENCE SUMMARY.
(Erase heading not required.)

Army Form C. 2118.

Place	Date	Hour	Summary of Events and Information	Remarks and references to Appendices

D. D. & L., London, E.C. Sch. 52

Army Form C. 2118.

Instructions regarding War Diaries and Intelligence Summaries are contained in F. S. Regs., Part II. and the Staff Manual respectively. Title pages will be prepared in manuscript.

WAR DIARY
or
INTELLIGENCE SUMMARY.
(Erase heading not required.)

Place	Date	Hour	Summary of Events and Information	Remarks and references to Appendices
			Ref Sheet 57B S.W. 1/[illegible]	
MORTHO WOOD	7/10/18	9.40pm.	The 113 Inf Bde assembled in T.1.b & T.7.a in readiness to attack MORTHO WOOD & French systems beyond. The 13th R.W.F assembled just E in the western trench in T.1.c.	113 Inf Bde B.O. 358
"	8/10/18		Boundaries: Interbattalion was T.2c.0.0. to T3.c.5.5.	
			Objectives: Brigade: T.3.d.91.50 to N.34d.40.00. with support line between T.3.d.3.3 to T3.a.5.9.	
			The relative position of battalions was Right – 16th R.W.F. Left – 13th RWF Support 14th R.W.F.	
	8/10/18	0105	The Brigade advanced from their assembly positions under a creeping barrage which moved at the rate of 100x per 5 min: A.B & C Coys were in the front line while D Coy formed support. Strong opposition was met with in T.1.c where strong belts of wire greatly impeded progress. In the sunken road T2.a & d the battalion was held up for some time by heavy M.G. & rifle fire from VILLERS-OUTREAUX, & by M.G. fire & snipers from ANGLES CHATEAU. A 77mm. battery from T.9.a.2.0, firing over open sights, caused considerable annoyance to our troops. ANGLES CHATEAU was reported in our hands at 0427 hrs. The opposition was overcome at 11.05 hr. & the final objective at T3b.30.90. – T3d.9.8 was reached. The two tanks at the disposal of the Brigade	13th Bn. Op. Ord. No 3

[illegible] Lt Col

D. D. & L., London, E.C. A5003) Wt. W1 71/M2031 750,000 5/17 Sch. 52 Forms/C2118/14

Army Form C. 2118.

Instructions regarding War Diaries and Intelligence Summaries are contained in F. S. Regs., Part II. and the Staff Manual respectively. Title pages will be prepared in manuscript.

WAR DIARY
or
INTELLIGENCE SUMMARY.
(Erase heading not required.)

Place	Date	Hour	Summary of Events and Information	Remarks and references to Appendices

D. D. & L., London, E.C. Wt. W. 3291/Forms/C. 2118/14

Army Form C. 2118.

WAR DIARY
or
INTELLIGENCE SUMMARY.
(Erase heading not required.)

Instructions regarding War Diaries and Intelligence Summaries are contained in F. S. Regs., Part II. and the Staff Manual respectively. Title pages will be prepared in manuscript.

Map Ref. 57B 1/40,000 & 57B S.W. 1/20,000. — October —

Place	Date	Hour	Summary of Events and Information	Remarks and references to Appendices
(Continued).	(Continued)		Batt. H.Q. was established first in S.12 C.9.7. & later at T.1.C.4.9.	
	8/10/18	2.45 pm	Batt. moved to banks in N.35.a. (N. of MALLINCOURT) and bivouaced for the night	
MALLINCOURT.	9/10/18	–	Batt rested during the morning.	
		4 pm.	Batt. moved to billets in MALLINCOURT.	
"	10/10/18	4 pm	Draft of 1 off. & 92 O.R. arrived: Day was spent in reorganizing the Companies.	
		5 pm	Battalion Concert.	
"	11/10/18	–	Training	
"	12/10/18	–	Battalion moved to BERTRY. Move was made across Country & in artillery formation. BERTRY was reached at 1300 hrs. Billets were provided in eastern end of Village	
BERTRY.	13/10/18	–	Training – Tactical Scheme in P.3 & P.10. Church Parades.	
"	14/10/18	–	Training – Tactical Scheme in P.3 & P.10.	
"	15/10/18	–	" in vicinity of billets	
		4-30 pm	Party reconnoitred crossings of R. SELLE in K22a with a view to attacking high grounds beyond.	J.F. Lemon? Lt Col

D. D. & L., London, E.C. A5003) Wt. W1 71/M2931 750,000 5/17 Sch. 52 Forms/C2118/14

Army Form C. 2118.

WAR DIARY

or

INTELLIGENCE SUMMARY.

(Erase heading not required.)

Instructions regarding War Diaries and Intelligence Summaries are contained in F. S. Regs., Part II. and the Staff Manual respectively. Title pages will be prepared in manuscript.

Place	Date	Hour	Summary of Events and Information	Remarks and references to Appendices

Instructions regarding War Diaries and Intelligence Summaries are contained in F. S. Regs., Part II. and the Staff Manual respectively. Title pages will be prepared in manuscript.

Army Form C. 2118.

WAR DIARY
or
INTELLIGENCE SUMMARY. – October –

(Erase heading not required.)

Ref map: Sheet 57B NE

Place	Date	Hour	Summary of Events and Information	Remarks and references to Appendices
MONTAY	20/10/18	0200h	An artillery & M.G. barrage was opened on the railway embankment & the ground immediately in front of it. At the same time the battalion, operating in conjunction with troops on the left flank, left the assembly position with A & D Coys in the front line & B & C in rear. The formation adopted was sections in column, A & D companies constituting one double wave, while B & C formed a second. Considerable opposition was encountered on the railway from M.Gs & rifles but this was speedily overcome, & the enemy surrendered freely. At the southern end of the orchards in K16d. B & C Coys passed through the leading wave, & meeting with only slight opposition, swept on to the final objective. Consolidation was at once begun on the two objectives. Two strong points were dug by a platoon of the 19th Bn Welsh Regt. (Pioneers) at K17c.8.2. & at K17.c.4.4. The 10th Bn R.W.F formed a defensive flank on our right along the MONTAY – FORREST RD. Casualties:	

	Killed	Wounded	Missing
Officers	× 1	1	—
O. Rank	* 8	47	—

+ 2Lt. E. J. Hughes
* " G. H. Thomas

Prisoners Captured — — 45 O Rank
Machine Guns — — 15
Trench Mortars — — 2

J. F. Leman Lt Col

D. D. & L., London, E.C. A5001) Wt. W1 71/M2031 750,000 5/17 Sch. 52 Forms/C2118/14

Army Form C. 2118.

WAR DIARY
or
INTELLIGENCE SUMMARY.
(Erase heading not required.)

Instructions regarding War Diaries and Intelligence Summaries are contained in F. S. Regs., Part II, and the Staff Manual respectively. Title pages will be prepared in manuscript.

Place	Date	Hour	Summary of Events and Information	Remarks and references to Appendices

Army Form C. 2118.

WAR DIARY
or
INTELLIGENCE SUMMARY. — October —

Instructions regarding War Diaries and Intelligence Summaries are contained in F. S. Regs., Part II. and the Staff Manual respectively. Title pages will be prepared in manuscript.

Ref Map Sheet 57B NE 1/...

(Erase heading not required.)

Place	Date	Hour	Summary of Events and Information	Remarks and references to Appendices
POIX du NORD.	28/10/18	–	Training in trench duties & handling of Lewis Gun.	
"	29/10/18	–	" " " " " " The following award was notified :– M.C. Rev. W. F. CROSTHWAIT, A.C.D.	
"	30/10/18	–	in the neighbourhood of Posts. Battalion was relieved by 14th Bn R.W.F. & moved to support positions in line running N.W. & S.E. through F.9 central. Batt. H.Q. F 8 d.0.4. Relief complete 1725 hrs.	
	31/10/18	–	Two left front Coys. moved to position in F.14 b. owing to heavy hostile shelling of original positions.	

J. F. Leman Lt Col.
Commanding 13th Battn. R.W.F.

D. D. & L., London, E.C.
A5005) Wt. W1 71/M2031 750,000 5/17 Sch. 52 Forms/C2118/14

13th RWF Vol 36

War Diary

for

November 1918

Instructions regarding War Diaries and Intelligence Summaries are contained in F. S. Regs., Part II. and the Staff Manual respectively. Title pages will be prepared in manuscript.

WAR DIARY
or
~~INTELLIGENCE SUMMARY.~~ November —

Army Form C. 2118.

Map Ref. Sheet 57 B /40000 (Erase heading not required.)

Place	Date	Hour	Summary of Events and Information	Remarks and references to Appendices
POIX du NORD (Bivouacs)	1st	–	Companies carried out training in Lewis Gun. Bn. H.Q. moved to F.9.b.	
"	2nd	9am to noon	Bn. carried out Tactical Scheme – attack through VENDEGIES WOOD	
"	3rd	–	General inspection of Equipment & Company Stores & overhauling of same. Resting remainder of the afternoon.	
"	4th	2am	Reveille was at 2am. A hot breakfast was served and the battalion moved off to the line at 3am. Companies moved independently to their assembly positions in front of ENGLEFONTAINE. The barrage of the 17th Divn attacking on our left opened at 5.30am and drew a certain amount of retaliatory on to the assembly positions and a few casualties were suffered. Companies were reported in position at 5.45 am. At 6-15 am the 115 Inf Bde left their assembly positions and met considerable opposition on the fringe of the FOREST de MORMAL. With the assistance of a tank this was overcome, & the battalion left its assembly position. A Coy was on the left, C Coy Centre – D Coy Right, while B Coy was in Right Support. Crossing the orchards in A.2 b & d all Companies were severely harassed by machine gun fire & by batteries firing at very close range. Very little determined resistance was encountered in spite of the numerous batches of enemy who were still hiding in the undergrowth, and the Companies swept to their first objectives in schedule time. A line was consolidated along the road running from A.4 b 95.40 to the road junction in A.10.a	

J. F. Leeman Lt Col.

D. D. & L., London, E.C. A5o2.) Wt. W1 71/M2031 750,000 5/17 Sch. 52 Forms/C2118/14

Army Form C. 2118.

WAR DIARY
or
INTELLIGENCE SUMMARY.
(Erase heading not required.)

Instructions regarding War Diaries and Intelligence Summaries are contained in F. S. Regs., Part II. and the Staff Manual respectively. Title pages will be prepared in manuscript.

Place	Date	Hour	Summary of Events and Information	Remarks and references to Appendices
[illegible]	[illegible]		[illegible]	

D. D. & L. London, E.C. Sch. 53 Forms C2118/4

Army Form C. 2118.

WAR DIARY
or
INTELLIGENCE SUMMARY. November —

Instructions regarding War Diaries and Intelligence Summaries are contained in F. S. Regs., Part II. and the Staff Manual respectively. Title pages will be prepared in manuscript. Map Ref 57A 1/40000 + 51 1/40000 (Erase heading not required.)

Place	Date	Hour	Summary of Events and Information	Remarks and references to Appendices
DOURLERS.	8th		carried out by the 14th & 16th RWF during the night & the line was advanced to the MAUBEUGE – AVESNES RD	
	"	3pm	– A minor operation was carried out by D Coy. which resulted in the taking of LA BELLE HOTESSE FM. The farm was evidently held strongly by the enemy, but on the advance of our troops the enemy fled, & our casualties were 5 men wounded.	
		5pm	At 5pm a light barrage was put on the road running N & S. through W86 central, by our artillery, & A Coy advanced to this line, without any resistance. A constant barrage was kept up by the enemy on the MAUBEUGE — AVESNES RD. particularly the portion in W.35.d & D12.c. This died down at 6.30 pm. and no more firing of any kind was heard on the part of the enemy.	
		9pm	A & D Coys advanced through the wood in W.36 + W.37 & patrols reached the edge of the wood & reported no trace of the enemy.	
WATTIGNIES	9th	6am.	– The battalion assembled at E4 central & along with troop of Oxford Hussars formed the advance guard of the Division. # Cavalry scouts reported the village of WATTIGNIES clear of the enemy at 7am & the battalion moved forward & threw out an outpost line along the stream in X25. Cavalry scouts reported no trace of the enemy in DIMONT – DIMECHAUX. or SOLRINNES. At 12-30pm. the 16 RWF passed through WATTIGNIES & took up an outpost line in front	# [illegible] assumed temporary command of the battalion in the absence of C.O. with [illegible]

J. F. Leman [illegible]

D. D. & L., London, E.C. (A8031) Wt. W1 71/M2031 750,000 5/17 Sch. 52 Forms/C2118/14

Instructions regarding War Diaries and Intelligence Summaries are contained in F. S. Regs., Part II. and the Staff Manual respectively. Title pages will be prepared in manuscript.

WAR DIARY
or
INTELLIGENCE SUMMARY.
(Erase heading not required.)

Army Form C. 2118.

Place	Date	Hour	Summary of Events and Information	Remarks and references to Appendices
WATTIGNIES	9th		[illegible] —	
			[illegible] billets in WATTIGNIES	
	10	–	[illegible] — Church Parade —	
"	11th	–	Cleaning [illegible] & inspection — of kit & equipment	
"	12th	–	— [illegible]	
"	13th		" " " "	
	14th		" " " "	
	15th	–	[illegible] DIMONT – DIMECHAUX – WATTIGNIES	
	16th	–	[illegible] WATTIGNIES	
	17th	–	[illegible]	
	18	–	[illegible]	
"	19	–	[illegible]	
			[illegible]	
"	20	–	[illegible] inspected by [illegible]	
	21	–	[illegible]	
			[illegible]	
			[illegible] BEAUFORT, LA HAUTE BORNE & BELLE HOTESSE Fm	
			[illegible]	

J. Fleman Lt Col

D. D. & L., London, E.C. [illegible] Sch. 52 Forms/C. 2118/4

Army Form C. 2118.

Instructions regarding War Diaries and Intelligence Summaries are contained in F. S. Regs., Part II. and the Staff Manual respectively. Title pages will be prepared in manuscript.

Map Sheet. 57.C/1. 57A/40000

WAR DIARY
or
INTELLIGENCE SUMMARY.
(Erase heading not required.)

— November —

Place	Date	Hour	Summary of Events and Information	Remarks and references to Appendices
WATTIGNIES.	23rd	—	Battalion marched via FLOURSIES – DOURLERS – POT DE VIN — AULNOYE & BERLIAMONT to SARBARAS. Dinners were taken on the way at LA TOQUE. SARBARAS was reached at 2-45 pm. & the battalion was billeted by 3-15 pm	
SARBARAS	24th	—	— Training in accordance with Programme & Church parades	
"	25th	—	— " " " " "	
"	26th	—	— " " " " "	
"	27th	—	— " " " " " Inter-battalion Rugby match. 13th RWs V. 16th RWs Result – 13th RWs. – 12 pts. 16th RWs – 6 pts	
"	28th	—	Training in accordance with Programme	
"	29th	—	Inter"-battalion" association" football match" – 13th RWs – V. 14th RWs. Result – 14th RWs – 2 – 13th RWs — 0.	
"	30	—	Training in accordance with Programme	

N. F. Keenan Lt. Col.

D. D. & L., London, E.C. A5003) Wt. W1 71/M2031 750,000 5/17 Sch. 52 Forms/C2118/14

13th R.W.F. Vol 37

WAR DIARY

FOR

DECEMBER 1918

Army Form C. 2118.

WAR DIARY
or
INTELLIGENCE SUMMARY.
(Erase heading not required.)

Instructions regarding War Diaries and Intelligence Summaries are contained in F. S. Regs., Part II. and the Staff Manual respectively. Title pages will be prepared in manuscript.

Map Sheet 57A 1/40000

December 1918

Place	Date	Hour	Summary of Events and Information	Remarks and references to Appendices
SARBARAS	1		Church Parades	
"	2		Training in accordance with programme	
"	3		Battalion proceeded by march route to C 11 d 3.8 and at 1100 hours formed up on the side of the road whilst H. M. The King proceeded down the lines.	
"	4		Training in accordance with programme	
"	5		Rugby Competition "2nd Round" 13th RWF "versus" Field Ambulance Result: Field Amb. 24 pts. 13th RWF Nil.	
"	6		Training in accordance with programme. LT. G.W. TAYLOR, 2/LTS H.R. MORGAN, W CLIFF, & J. C. PALMER joined for duty.	
"	7		Training in accordance with programme. Final Brigade Assoc. Football competition. Result: 16th RWF beat 14th RWF.	
"	8		Church Parades	

J. F. Leman Lt Col

D. D. & L., London, E.C. (A8001) Wt. W1 71/M2031 750,000 5/17 Sch. 52 Forms/C2118/14

Instructions regarding War Diaries and Intelligence Summaries are contained in F. S. Regs., Part II. and the Staff Manual respectively. Title pages will be prepared in manuscript.

WAR DIARY
or
INTELLIGENCE SUMMARY.
(Erase heading not required.)

Army Form C. 2118.

December [illegible]

Place	Date	Summary of Events and Information	Remarks and references to Appendices
[illegible]	9th	Training in accordance with programme	
"	10	" " " " "	
"	11	" " " " "	
"	12	" " " " "	
"	13	" " " " "	
"	14	" " " " "	
"	15	Church Parades	
	16	Training in accordance with programme	

Army Form C. 2118.

WAR DIARY
or
INTELLIGENCE SUMMARY.
(Erase heading not required.)

Instructions regarding War Diaries and Intelligence Summaries are contained in F. S. Regs., Part II. and the Staff Manual respectively. Title pages will be prepared in manuscript.

Map Sheet 57c 1/40000

December 1918

Place	Date	Hour	Summary of Events and Information	Remarks and references to Appendices
SARBARAS	17		Training in accordance with programme Military Medal awarded to Ptes S. Hice, R. Jones, V Gildersleeve, T Whelan.	
"	18		Training in accordance with programme	
"	19		Inspection of the Battalion by the Commanding Officer. 10.30 hrs Route March.	
"	20		Inspection of the Battalion by the Brigadier General Commanding	
"	21		Training in accordance with programme.	
"	22		Church Parades Brigade Tug of War Competition in the afternoon Result First round: 13th RWF beat 16th RWF in two pulls Final : 13th RWF " 14th RWF " " "	
"	23		Training in accordance with programme.	

J F Leman? Lt Col

D. D. & L., London, E.C.
(A5093) Wt. W1 71/M2031 750,000 5/17 Sch. 52 Forms/C2118/14

Army Form C. 2118.

WAR DIARY
or
INTELLIGENCE SUMMARY.
(Erase heading not required.)

Instructions regarding War Diaries and Intelligence Summaries are contained in F. S. Regs., Part II. and the Staff Manual respectively. Title pages will be prepared in manuscript.

Map Sheet 57^c 1/40000

December 1918

Place	Date	Hour	Summary of Events and Information	Remarks and references to Appendices
[illegible]	24		Battalion Route March. Afternoon Brigade Boxing Competition. Winners: 13th RWF.	
"	25		Christmas Day. Church Services in the morning. Afternoon & evening Mens dinners.	
"	26		General cleaning up of equipment & billeting area.	
	[illegible]		[illegible] billets there at 13.00 hours.	
[illegible]	[illegible]		The Battalion [illegible] paraded at 09.05 hours by march route to INCHY [illegible] in Billets there at 13.30 hours.	
INCHY	[illegible]		The Battalion less Transport embussed at 08.30 hours & proceeded to billets at FRAMERVILLE arriving there at 15.00 hours	
FRAMERVILLE	30		General cleaning up of billeting area & allotment of messes & offices	
	31		1½ hours training & general cleaning of area continued.	

[signature] Lt Col.

Army Form C. 2118. Sch 52 Forms/C2118/14

38 P+F

13TH BATTN ROYAL WELSH FUSRS
Vol 38

WAR DIARY

FOR

JANUARY - 1919

38B
5 sheets

WAR DIARY
or
INTELLIGENCE SUMMARY — January 1919 —
(*Erase heading not required.*)

Army Form C. 2118.

Instructions regarding War Diaries and Intelligence Summaries are contained in F. S. Regs., Part II. and the Staff Manual respectively. Title pages will be prepared in manuscript.

Place	Date	Hour	Summary of Events and Information	Remarks and references to Appendices
FRAMERIES	1/1/19	—	Training in accordance with programme & work on the Battn area. Repairing of Billets Etc	
"	2/1/19	—	Training in accordance with programme & work in the Battalion area	
"	3/1/19	—	Training in accordance with programme & work in the Battalion area. Temp Lieut W.G. Calwell 13th R.F. to be acting Captain whilst Commanding a Company 19.11.18	
"	4/1/19	—	Training in accordance with programme & work on Battalion area. Capt G.R. Pater M.C. assumes command of "C" Coy vice Capt R.H. Wynne-Edwards D.S.O. M.C. (leave to England). Regimental Censorship of letters discontinued	
"	5/1/19	—	Church Services in accordance with programme	
"	6/1/19	—	Training in accordance with programme	
	7/1/19	—	Battalion route march and training in accordance with programme. Inspection of transport by Divisional General	Lt

J F [illegible]
Commanding
13th R. [illegible]

D. D. & L., London, E.C. A.(?) Wt. [illegible] 750,000 5/17 Sch. 52 Forms/C2118/14

Army Form C. 2118.

Instructions regarding War Diaries and Intelligence Summaries are contained in F. S. Regs., Part II. and the Staff Manual respectively. Title pages will be prepared in manuscript.

WAR DIARY
or
INTELLIGENCE SUMMARY. — January – 1919 —
(*Erase heading not required.*)

Place	Date	Hour	Summary of Events and Information	Remarks and references to Appendices
FRANVILLERS	8/1/19	–	Battalion route march and training in accordance with programme	
"	9/1/19	–	Battalion route march and work on the Battalion area.	
"	10/1/19	–	Battalion route march and training in accordance with programme	
"	11/1/19	–	Adjutants parade and training in accordance with Programme.	
			2nd Lt J. C. Palmer will assume the duties of A/Quartermaster from today	
"	12/1/19	–	Church services in accordance with programme	
"	13/1/19	–	Battalion route march and training in accordance with programme	
"	14/1/19	–	Adjutant's parade and work on Battalion area	
"	15/1/19	–	Adjutant's parade and work on Battalion area	
	"		Captain G.F. Fitz-Gerald M.C. & Lieut C.W. Coulter MC proceeded to England for demobilization	
"	16/1/19	–	Training in accordance with programme and presentation of Colours by G.O.C.	

J F Lennon [illegible]
Commanding
B.B. [illegible]

D. D. & L., London, E.C. (A8023) Wt. W1 71/M2031 750,000 5/17 Sch. 52 Forms/C2118/14

Instructions regarding War Diaries and Intelligence Summaries are contained in F. S. Regs., Part II. and the Staff Manual respectively. Title pages will be prepared in manuscript.

WAR DIARY
or
INTELLIGENCE SUMMARY.
(Erase heading not required.)

January 1919 —

Army Form C. 2118.

Place	Date	Hour	Summary of Events and Information	Remarks and references to Appendices
FRANVILLERS	17/1	—	Battalion parade for reception of Kings Colours and work in Batt. area parade interfered with by weather conditions	
"	18/1	—	Battalion Parade for reception of Kings Colours and work in Batt. area.	
	19/1	—	Church [illegible] in accordance with Programme. 2/Lt. [illegible] Stawell A.C. transferred to B Coy	
"	20/1	—	Battalion route march and work in Battalion area.	
"	[illegible]	—	[illegible] parade and training in accordance with Programme.	
"	[illegible]	—	[illegible] in accordance with [illegible] and work in Battalion area. Brigade inter-company [illegible] Soccer Competition [illegible] V A. Coy 16th R.W.F. Result 13th 4 goals 16th 1 goal	
"	[illegible]	—	Battalion route march and work in Battalion area. Tug of war [illegible] Competition 13th R.W.F. V 16th R.W.F. result win for R.W.F.	
"	[illegible]	—	[illegible] parade and training in accordance with Programme.	

[illegible signature]

D. D. & L., London, E.C.
[illegible] Sch. 52 Forms C2118/14

Army Form C. 2118.

Instructions regarding War Diaries and Intelligence Summaries are contained in F. S. Regs., Part II. and the Staff Manual respectively. Title pages will be prepared in manuscript.

WAR DIARY
or
INTELLIGENCE SUMMARY.
(*Erase heading not required.*) — January 1919 —

Place	Date	Hour	Summary of Events and Information	Remarks and references to Appendices
FRANVILLERS	25/1/19	–	Battalion route march and work on Battalion area.	
"	26/1/19	–	Church Services in accordance with programme.	
			Inter-Battalion team Push-Bike-race — Cancelled on account of weather.	
"	27/1/19	–	Adjutant's parade and training in accordance with programme	
			Court-Martial on No 91518 Pte F Barker. 13th R.W.F.	
			Tug of War (Divisional Competition) 13th R.W.F. V 17th R.W.F. result win for 17th R.W.F.	
			Final inter-Company Soccer Competition "B" Coy 13th R.W.F. V "C" Coy. 16th R.W.F	
			Result "C" Coy 16th R.W.F. 4 goals, B Coy 13th R.W.F. 1 goal	
"	28/1/19	–	Tug of War (Final) in Divnl Competition. 13th Bn. V. 17th Bn. —	
			Result. 17th Bn. R.W.F. 2 pulls — 13th Bn. NIL.	
"	29/1/19	–	Final in Divnl. Boxing competition at WARLOY. Teams 13th Bn. & 2nd Bn. R.W.F. — Result. 13th Bn. 15 pts. 2nd Bn. — 5½ pts.	
"	30/1/19	–	Training & work in accordance with programme.	
"	31/1/19	–	" " " " " " "	

[Signature] Lt Col
Commanding
13th Bn. R.W. Fus.

D. D. & L., London, E.C.
(A8023) Wt. W1 71/M2031 750,000 5/17 Sch. 52 Forms/C2118/14

Instructions regarding War Diaries and Intelligence Summaries are contained in F. S. Regs., Part II. and the Staff Manual respectively. Title pages will be prepared in manuscript.

WAR DIARY
or
INTELLIGENCE SUMMARY.
(Erase heading not required.)

Army Form C. 2118.

13 RWF

FEBRUARY

98 39

Place	Date	Hour	Summary of Events and Information	Remarks and references to Appendices
Franvillers nr. AMIENS	1.2.19	-	Church Parades	
	2.2.19	-	Companies paraded at 9.30am under Coy Commanders for short route march. Coys were amalgamated – "A" & "B" Coys forming "No. 1 Coy" and "C" & "D" Coys "No. 2 Coy". The No. 1 Coy to be under the Command of Capt G.R. PATON M.C. and No. 2 Coy under the Command of Capt W.E. ATWELL.	
	3.2.19		9.30am – 10am Physical training; 10am – 10.30am Rapid march under Coy Commanders. 10.30am – 12.30pm Overhauling & oiling Lewis Guns. Sports:- A push bike race under Div'l arrangements was held during the afternoon. Distance 12 miles. Starting point ALBERT; Finishing point PONT NOYELLES.	
	4.2.19		9.30 – 10am Physical Training; 10 – 11.30am Route march in [illegible] dress under Coy Commanders. 11.30 – 12noon Coys at disposal of Coy Commanders for [illegible] & gathering fuel.	
	6.2.19		H.R.H. the Prince of Wales visited this area about 11am and inspected the Battalion. No special parade was held, but H.R.H. inspected & chatted with the men while they were at work. [illegible] 9.30am P.T.; 9.45 – 10.15am Short Route March. 10.15 – 12.30. Fatigues.	
	7.2.19		Coys paraded as strong as possible for Route March in Drill Order (without rifles) under Capt G.R. Paton, M.C.	
	8.2.19		Church Parades.	
	9.2.19		9.30/10am P.T. 2 – 4pm Baths.	
	10.2.19		No. 1 and 2 Coys were combined to form one Company under the command of Capt G.R. Paton M.C. 9.30am Coy Route March under Coy Comndr. Dress Drill Order (without rifles).	

[signature]
Comdg. 13th R.W.F.

D. D. & L., London, E.C.
A7093 Wt. W4 [illegible] 750,000 5/17 Sch. 52 Forms/C.2118/14

Instructions regarding War Diaries and Intelligence Summaries are contained in F. S. Regs., Part II. and the Staff Manual respectively. Title pages will be prepared in manuscript.

WAR DIARY
or
INTELLIGENCE SUMMARY.
(Erase heading not required.)

FEBRUARY

Army Form C. 2118.

Place	Date	Hour	Summary of Events and Information	Remarks and references to Appendices
FRANVILLERS NR. AMIENS.	11.2.19.		Company at the disposal of Capt Paton for inspection & Physical training. At 12.15 pm. the draft of 40 O.R's selected for Army of Occupation paraded for inspection by the G.O.C, 38th (Welsh) Division.	
"	12.2.19		Draft of 40 O.R's for A of O. paraded for inspection of kit requipment. Remainder – cleaning kit requipment – Physical Drill.	
"	13.2.19.		Bn paraded as strong as possible under O.C. Coy for Route March – Dress Drill order without rifle. A "fall out" was given at QUERRIEU so that men may visit the Chateau to see the Divisional Shield made by the Divnl R.E's and dedicated to H.R.H The Prince of Wales.	
"	14.2.19		Parades:- 9.30/10 am. P.T; 10am – 12.30 pm Cleaning all Lewis Guns &c. In the evening a Cinema performance was given in the large Recreation Hut.	
"	15.2.19.		~~Church Parades~~ Normal Routine – Another Cinema performance was given during the evening	
"	16.2.19		Church Parades. Draft of 15 O.Rs (Army of Occupation) left Bn at 2.15 pm & proceeded to HESDIN for work under the E.F. Canteens	
"	17.2.19.		During the morning men were employed on fatigue. Afternoon – bathing.	
"	18.2.19		" " " " " "	
"	19.2.19.		" " " " " Afternoon – bathing parades.	
"	20.2.19.		The Draft of 40 O.R's for Army of Occupation left the Bn. at 9.15 am. & proceeded to DUNKIRK AREA to join the 26th Bn. R.W.F. – 59th Division.	
"	21.2.19		During the morning men were at work on Bn. area	
"	22.2.19		" " " " " "	
	23.2.19		Church Parade.	

[illegible]
Major

D. D. & L., London, E.C.
A5025) Wt. W1 71/M2031 750,000 5/17 Sch. 52 Forms/C2118/14

Instructions regarding War Diaries and Intelligence Summaries are contained in F. S. Regs., Part II. and the Staff Manual respectively. Title pages will be prepared in manuscript.

WAR DIARY
or
INTELLIGENCE SUMMARY.
(Erase heading not required.)

FEBRUARY

Army Form C. 2118.

Place	Date	Hour	Summary of Events and Information	Remarks and references to Appendices
FRANVILLERS Nr AMIENS	24/2/19		Morning, men at work on [illegible] area; Afternoon Bathing parade	
"	25/2/19		" " " " " " " "	
"	26/2/19		Men employed on fatigues	
"	27/2/19		" " "	
"	28/2/19		182 O.R. (Army of occupation) left the Bn at 13.00 hours and proceeded to II Corps Concentration Camp.	

J [illegible]
Major [illegible] Bn

D. D. & L., London, E.C.
Army Wt W 1 21 M/1917 750,000 5/17 Sch 52 Forms/C2118/14

Instructions regarding War Diaries and Intelligence Summaries are contained in F. S. Regs., Part II. and the Staff Manual respectively. Title pages will be prepared in manuscript.

WAR DIARY
or
INTELLIGENCE SUMMARY. MARCH Vol 40
(Erase heading not required.)

Army Form C. 2118.

Place	Date 1919	Hour	Summary of Events and Information	Remarks and references to Appendices
[illegible]	1st		St David's Day. Lt Col J. F. [illegible] DSO went on leave. Major J. A. Wilson M.C. assumed command of the battalion.	
	2		Church parade	
	3		Fatigues in and around billets. Afternoon baths	
	4			
	5			
	6			
	7			
	8			
	9		Bathing parade	
	10		Fatigues in and around billets + baths	

J. [illegible] Major
Commanding 13th RWF

40 B
3 [illegible]

D. D. & L., London, E.C.
(A10266) Wt W3300/P713 750,000 2/18 Sch. 52 Forms/C2118/16

Army Form C. 2118.

WAR DIARY
or
INTELLIGENCE SUMMARY.
(Erase heading not required.)

Instructions regarding War Diaries and Intelligence Summaries are contained in F. S. Regs., Part II. and the Staff Manual respectively. Title pages will be prepared in manuscript.

Place	Date	Hour	Summary of Events and Information	Remarks and references to Appendices

D. D. & L., London, E.C.
A10260 Wt W5300/P713 750,000 2/16 Sch. 52 Forms/C2118/10

Army Form C. 2118.

Instructions regarding War Diaries and Intelligence Summaries are contained in F. S. Regs., Part II. and the Staff Manual respectively. Title pages will be prepared in manuscript.

WAR DIARY
or
INTELLIGENCE SUMMARY. — MARCH —
(Erase heading not required.)

Place	Date	Hour	Summary of Events and Information	Remarks and references to Appendices
BLANGY-TRONVILLE	22/3/19	–	Fatigue duties and General cleaning up of Camp	
	23/3/19	–	Church Parades	
	24/3/19	–	General cleaning of equipment and inspections. Fatigue duties around Camp.	
	25/3/19	–	" " " " " "	
	26/3/19	–	Inspection of men. Fatigues + Recreational Training	
	27/3/19	–	" " " " " "	
	28/3/19	–	" " " " " " – Baths	
	29/3/19	–	Gen Du Pree commanding 38th Div. Cadre inspected the Camp	
	30/3/19	–	Church Parade	
	31/3/19	–	Cleaning of Camp – Fuel Collecting parties – Inspection of men	

[illegible] Major
Commanding 13 RWF

D. D. & L., London, E.C.
(A10266) Wt W5300/P713 750,000 2/18 Sch. 52 Forms/C2118/16

13 RWF

Army Form C. 2118.

Instructions regarding War Diaries and Intelligence Summaries are contained in F. S. Regs., Part II. and the Staff Manual respectively. Title pages will be prepared in manuscript.

WAR DIARY
or
INTELLIGENCE SUMMARY. — April — Vol 41

(Erase heading not required.)

Place	Date	Hour 1919	Summary of Events and Information	Remarks and references to Appendices
[illegible]	1st		Camp fatigues Sorting & cleaning of Stores & Equipment	
	2		[illegible]	
	3		[illegible]	
	4		[illegible]	
	5		[illegible]	
	6th		Church Parades	
	7th		Camp fatigues	
	8		[illegible] carried out [illegible] ROVES	
	9		Camp fatigues	
	10th		[illegible]	
	11		"	
	12		"	
	13		Church Parades	
	14th		[illegible] carried out [illegible]	
	15th		BRETTONEUX [illegible] DAC	
			[illegible]	
	16th		[illegible]	
	17		" " Result no [illegible]	[illegible]

D. D. & L., London, E.C.
(A10990) Wt. W5300/P713 750,000 2/16 Sch. 52 Forms/C2118/16

Instructions regarding War Diaries and Intelligence Summaries are contained in F. S. Regs., Part II. and the Staff Manual respectively. Title pages will be prepared in manuscript.

WAR DIARY
or
INTELLIGENCE SUMMARY. April —

(*Erase heading not required.*)

Army Form C. 2118.

Place	Date	Hour	Summary of Events and Information	Remarks and references to Appendices
[illegible] – [illegible]	18th		Church Parade & Camp Fatigues	
	19th		Camp fatigues — [illegible] of [illegible] [illegible] 113th Bde. [illegible] [illegible] [illegible] 113th Bde. [illegible]	
	20th		Church Parades	
	21		[illegible]	
			[illegible]	
	22		Camp fatigues	
	23			
	24			
	25	"	Camp fatigues	
	27	"	Church Parades	
	28	"	[illegible] M.C. [illegible] Command [illegible] 17th R.W.F. [illegible] [illegible] to Camp [illegible]	
	29		Camp fatigues	
	30	"	" "	

J. H. [illegible] Lt Col
Comd. 13th R.W.F.

[illegible]

D. D. & L., London, E.C.
(A10266) Wt W5300/P713 750,000 2/18 Sch. 52 Forms/C2118/16